W9-ASO-273

The Andrew R. Cecil Lectures on Moral Values in a Free Society

established by

The University of Texas at Dallas

Volume IX

Previous Volumes of the Andrew R. Cecil Lectures
on Moral Values in a Free Society

Volume I: The Third Way (1979)
Volume II: The Ethics of Citizenship (1980)
Volume III: Conflict and Harmony (1981)
Volume IV: The Search for Justice (1982)
Volume V: The Citizen and His Government (1983)
Volume VI: Our Freedoms: Rights and
    Responsibilities (1984)
Volume VII: A Melting Pot or a Nation
    of Minorities (1985)
Volume VIII: Traditional Moral Values in the Age
    of Technology (1986)

The Foundations of a Free Society
    by Andrew R. Cecil
Three Sources of National Strength
    by Andrew R. Cecil

DEMOCRACY:
ITS STRENGTHS AND WEAKNESSES

Democracy: Its Strengths and Weaknesses

CHARLES B. RENFREW
WILLIAM LEE MILLER
PATRICK E. HIGGINBOTHAM
GEORGE A. BIRRELL
ANDREW R. CECIL

With an Introduction by
ANDREW R. CECIL

Edited by
W. LAWSON TAITTE

The University of Texas at Dallas
1988

ST. PHILIP'S COLLEGE LIBRARY

Copyright © 1988 by The University of Texas at Dallas
All Rights Reserved
Printed in the United States of America

Library of Congress Catalog Card Number 88-050276
International Standard Book Number 0-292-71557-9

Distributed by the University of Texas Press,
Box 7819, Austin, Texas 78712

ST PHILIP'S COLLEGE LIBRARY

FOREWORD

In 1979, The University of Texas at Dallas established the Andrew R. Cecil Lectures on Moral Values in a Free Society in order to provide a forum for the discussion of the important issues that face our society. Each year since then the University has invited leading statesmen and scholars to its campus to share their ideas with the academic community and the general public, and this series has become a valued tradition for this institution and the community. The prominent authorities in many fields who have participated in the Lectures have contributed positively to our understanding of the system of moral values on which our country was founded, so that in offering the Lectures on Moral Values in a Free Society the University is discharging an important obligation and trust.

The University named this program for Dr. Andrew R. Cecil, its Distinguished Scholar in Residence. During his tenure as President of The Southwestern Legal Foundation, Dr. Cecil's innovative leadership moved that institution into the forefront of continuing legal education in the United States. When he retired from the Foundation as its Chancellor Emeritus, Dr. Cecil was asked by The University of Texas at Dallas to serve as its Distinguished Scholar in Residence, and the Cecil Lectures were instituted. It is appropriate that they honor a man who has been concerned throughout his career with the moral foundations of our society and has stressed his belief in the dignity and worth of every individual.

The ninth annual series of the Cecil Lectures was held on the campus of the University on November 9 through 12, 1987. The theme of the 1987 Lectures

084870

was "Democracy: Its Strengths and Weaknesses." On behalf of The University of Texas at Dallas, I wish to express our gratitude to Judge Patrick E. Higginbotham, to Professor William Lee Miller, to Mr. Charles B. Renfrew, to Mr. George A. Birrell, and to Dr. Cecil for their willingness to share their ideas and for the outstanding lectures that are preserved in these proceedings.

U.T. Dallas also wishes to express its appreciation to all those who have helped make this program an important part of the life of the University, especially the contributors to the program. By their support these donors enable us to continue this important project and to publish the proceedings of the series, thus assuring a wide and permanent audience for the ideas they contain.

I know that everyone who reads *Democracy: Its Strengths and Weaknesses*, the Andrew R. Cecil Lectures on Moral Values in a Free Society Volume IX, will be stimulated by the ideas presented in the five lectures it contains.

ROBERT H. RUTFORD, President
The University of Texas at Dallas
March, 1988

CONTENTS

INTRODUCTION

by

Andrew R. Cecil

During World War II, the English writer known as George Orwell wrote a satire on revolutionary politics called *Animal Farm.* In this short book, which has become one of the classics of twentieth-century political literature, the animals on a farm take it over from the human beings who had owned it. After this revolution—which is marked by such slogans as "Four legs good, two legs bad"—there is a sense of a new day which has dawned for the downtrodden. A new morality is established among the animals, promulgated in the Seven Commandments (rather than Ten) written large in whitewash upon the barn wall. The egalitarian dream of a new age is typified by the seventh and greatest of these commandments, which is that "All animals are equal."

The utopian paradise of the farm run by and for the animals does not last long in Orwell's story. Almost as soon as the revolution has been accomplished, the greediest group of the animals, the pigs, slyly begin to run things for their own advantage. One by one, the animals awake to find the written commandments subtly altered and distorted. Finally only one commandment is left on the wall, and it now reads: "All animals are equal but some are more equal than others."

11

ST. PHILIP'S COLLEGE LIBRARY

Although Orwell's point in *Animal Farm* was the betrayal of revolutionary ideals by brutal dictators and their followers, such as Stalin and his cronies in the Soviet Union, there is a more general lesson to be learned from the alteration of the utopian slogan, which applies also to the political system known as democracy. Democracy is government by the people, but there has never been a society where all the people have exercised the same authority to govern.

In Greece, where the term "democracy" was invented, not all the citizens of Athens participated in the choice of the ruler or in the enactment of the laws. Pure democracy never existed in Greece. In Athens— often considered the cradle of democracy—not all the people had the capacity to act directly or through representatives to control the State's institutions. The rights of citizenship were exercised by fewer than half of the adult males in the population, with women, slaves, aliens, and outlanders being excluded.

An Athenian citizen was described as "one who takes part in judicial decisions, and in holding office." It was only Pericles, in his famous funeral oration celebrating the virtues of democracy, who claimed that capacity is the sole criterion for holding office. Other Greek thinkers denied this Periclean claim and found democracy that operated on the basis of the participation of "all" its citizens to be an inherently unstable form of government. They believed such an idea had no chance to become a practical reality.

More in harmony with the facts of Greek history was a system based on an aristocratic or oligarchic participation in making judicial decisions and in holding office. Plato warned against the ignorance of

ST. PHILIP'S COLLEGE LIBRARY

political leaders in a democracy and warned of the danger of a demagoguery that leads to tyranny. Because of the shortcomings he perceived in the democratic ideal, Plato rejected the concept of democracy, advocating in *The Republic* a system that combined what he saw as the best qualities of monarchy and aristocracy. Aristotle also had reservations about the idea of democracy, accepting it as the lesser of evils. He sought to combine aristocracy—the essence of which, he believed, is the "distribution of offices according to goodness"—with the will of the majority, which prevails in a democracy.

While Plato was afraid that the poor would always control a democracy, Aristotle envisioned good government in cities with a large middle class, which would have a "great steadying influence and check the opposing extremes" of the rich and the poor. He preferred to leave the practical matters of government in the hands of the wealthy, who could offer their time and talents to public affairs, but in order to preserve stability through moderation, Aristotle recommended a constitutional government or polity that combines the merits of democracy and oligarchy.

In Rome under the empire we can discern the trappings of various ideals of governmental structure—monarchy was represented by the consuls, aristocracy by the Senate, and democracy by the popular assemblies. But though the state was formally a *res publica*, a "public affair," the authority vested in the people implied by this term was as a rule ignored by the emperor. The concept of natural rights—a concept that is central to the idea of democracy—was, however, stressed by Cicero, who believed that such

natural rights are given by God to man for the promotion of his well-being and the satisfaction of his
fundamental needs.

The division of the Roman people into patricians
and plebeians became a source of serious conflicts.
Through compromise and political concessions, the
plebeians made constitutional gains that ended the
patrician-plebeian struggle. Throughout the history of
civilization, such divisions of society have repeatedly
arisen. Hindu civilization developed the caste system, separating its people into Brahmins, Kshatriyas,
Vaisyas, and Sudras—and leaving outside the Pariahs.
The society of feudal Europe was divided into
aristocrats, the mercantile middle class, artisans, and
peasants. Throughout the Western world—until the
nineteenth century, when the philosophy of democracy began to triumph—we see the traces of sharp
divisions between rich and poor, oppressors and
oppressed, the privileged nobility and the under-
privileged common man.

Even the American Experiment, which Thomas
Jefferson compared to a "ball of liberty" that would
"roll around the globe," at first addressed only the
right to liberty, leaving open the question of a form
of governance. The American Constitution, in its
original form, is rather silent on the subject of basic
human rights. It was the Bill of Rights that moved
the emerging United States toward the ideal of
democracy.

Those who wrote "We the People" were mostly
men of substance who felt that only the "well born"
could be entrusted with the responsibility of government. John Adams, in his suggestion of a bicameral

legislature, sought a balance between an "aristocracy" and the "common man." Although the word "slavery" was not mentioned in the Constitution, the practice of slavery was incorporated into the document. Justice William Brennan pointed out that: ". . . indeed, throughout much of the 19th century, the position of women in our society was, in many respects, comparable to that of blacks under the pre-Civil War slave codes. Neither slaves nor women could hold office, serve on juries, or bring suit in their own names . . ." (*Frontiero v. Richardson*, 411 U.S. 677, 685, 93 S.Ct. 1764, 1769 [1973].)

On many occasions it has been said that the Constitution is not a self-executing document. The understanding that our ancestors had of the First Amendment permitted the enactment of the Alien and Sedition Laws, that later disappeared from the books, and the Supreme Court decision of *Plessy v. Ferguson*, which was supplanted in 1954 by the Court's decision in the case of *Brown v. Board of Education of Topeka*. Let us mention some of the changes in the understanding of the Constitution that have taken place in our generation.

Was it the "original intent" of the framers of the Constitution to have a descendant of African slaves and a woman serve on the Supreme Court, or for a black man to run for the presidency of the United States? Was it within the realm of their "original intent" to outlaw school segregation, to require reapportionment along the lines of one person-one vote, to allow or disallow prayers in public schools, to endorse or overthrow the legalization of abortion? It seems that the Founding Fathers devoted the least amount of their concern, attention, and time to these and a number of other controversial questions that have arisen during the 200 years the Constitution has served our nation.

The Constitutional Convention could not end slavery. The Founding Fathers combined idealism with pragmatism. Had the Constitution included provisions for abolishing slavery, the Constitution would never have been adopted. It would not have been ratified by the required number, nine, of the thirteen states. The Constitution became a reality through compromises. The Founding Fathers did not have an aspiration to find solutions for all future realities and the needs of a changing world. They created a framework for future generations, which guided by the "spirit of the age" have the responsibility to put meaning into the Constitution, that otherwise would become a meaningless and hollow document.

The "spirit of the age" becomes determined by the character, the independence, the resolution, and the right purpose of the men and women who vote and choose the public servants of whom the government is to consist. As Justice Holmes pointed out in his *The Common Law*: "The life of the law has not been logic: it has been experience. The felt necessities of the time, the prevalent moral and political theories, intuitions of public policy, avowed or unconscious, even the prejudices which judges share with their fellow-men have had a good deal more to do than the syllogism in determining the rules by which men should be governed."

There will be disagreements in all attempts to discover the "spirit of the age." The framers of the Constitution disagreed vehemently among themselves about many issues—to mention only the controversies that raged between Alexander Hamilton and Jefferson, between Hamilton and James Madison, between Hamilton and Charles Pinckney, and even between the father of this nation—George Washington—and the father of the Constitution—James Madison. The 55 delegates who arrived at the Philadelphia Convention represented in their arduous debate of almost four months widely diverse and frequently conflicting views. Although some of the framers were slave owners (and though many among this group themselves hated slavery), the basic concept undergirding their thoughts was a belief in the worth and dignity of every human being.

The essence of democracy is the dignity of man. The framers left to posterity the interpretation of such ambiguous clauses—referred to by Justice Holmes as "magnificent generalities"—as "due process of law," "the common defense," and "the general welfare." The framers expected that in this process of interpretation later generations would be guided by the general tenor and object of the Constitution—which considers liberty as the essential working principle of government—but at the same time expected that the Constitution would permit the ideas of later generations, as Justice Holmes expressed it, to compete in the "market place."

Democracy, as Jefferson said, is "the only form of government which is not eternally at open or secret war with the rights of the people." Although under the Constitution these rights are the same for all, regardless of the occupation or the material resources of the individual, in reality wealth and social position remain tangible standards of social distinction. With growing acquisitions, mega-mergers, and hostile take-overs affecting thousands of human beings, the corporate management and business in general become a highly visible and vulnerable target for criticism. Accumulation of excessive or preponderant means of exercising political and economic control could cause the erosion of the idea of equality of opportunity, which is so indispensable for democracy.

Mr. Charles B. Renfrew, in his lecture in the 1987 lectures on Moral Values in a Free Society entitled "The Interaction of Business and Democracy in Our Political System," stresses this interdependence between economic liberty and political liberty. He points out that historically the one kind of freedom has not long continued to exist without the other. No country offers true self-government in the political arena without a large degree of economic choice, and no country with an economic system of free-market capitalism can long withstand the pressure for political and civil freedoms as well.

Mr. Renfrew finds the common origin of democracy and capitalism in the commitment to freedom and individualism, in the belief in equality before the law and in the principle that all individuals "have inherently the same worth with the same dignity."

We may ask: What is the source of this belief? The American colonies were founded upon the premise that nothing is more valuable than human dignity, which is derived from man's unique relationship to the Creator of the Universe. The early colonists subscribed to the political system known as democracy because democracy provided a favorable climate to the growth of this spiritual belief. Democracy was not the source of this belief. Man was meant to be free and to have the ability to stand unimpeded in the light of his Creator as he sees fit to discern that light.

The writers of the Declaration of Independence proclaimed the birth of our nation "with a firm reliance on the protection of Divine Providence." George Washington began his inaugural address with "fervent supplication to that Almighty Being who rules the Universe" and in his farewell address besought "the Almighty to avert or mitigate" whatever evils the new Republic might face. Abraham Lincoln prayed at Gettysburg "that this nation, under God, shall have a new birth of freedom."

In his lecture, "Some Underpinnings of American Constitutional Democracy," Professor William Lee Miller demonstrates that the elaborate system of checks and balances built into our system of government by the Constitution is based on a specific conception of humanity. This conception, which derived largely from the Reformed tradition of Christianity, emphasized not only the dignity of man but also his weakness—all must have a hand in the government, because no single individual is wise or good enough to be entrusted with all power.

The element of mistrust of human weakness that this religious tradition imparted to our constitutional system of government has been much discussed and well understood. Professor Miller also contends that there is also another element in our heritage from our forefathers that has been paid less respect in recent

years. This is the sense of community, of mutual striv-
ing toward a common goal, of a public discourse based
upon common values. Professor Miller ascribes the
remarkable successes in the history of our nation to a
democratic system based on such a principle of
mutual respect and human dignity.

The Declaration of Independence defines the
dignity and equality of human beings in terms of
"unalienable rights." Through the system of checks
and balances we have mentioned, the Constitution,
along with the Bill of Rights and the other Amendments, protect these "unalienable rights," based on
truths which are "self-evident," against both the executive and legislative branches of government. The
independent judiciary, headed by the United States
Supreme Court, has the power to declare the acts of
the other two branches of government unconstitutional, thus offering an "inpenetrable bulwark"
against any attempt to violate the individual rights
embodied in the Constitution.

Such an "inpenetrable bulwark" was envisioned by
James Madison when he proposed that "independent
tribunals of justice will consider themselves in a
manner the guardian of these rights; they will be an
inpenetrable bulwark against every assumption of
power in the legislative or executive." In 1803 in the
case of *Marbury v. Madison*, Chief Justice Marshall
established the doctrine of judicial review, which in
Marshall's words states: "It is emphatically the
province and duty of the judicial department to say
what the law is."

The Supreme Court, according to this doctrine, has
the final word on whether or not the law—an act of a

local or state government or of the Congress or an Executive Decree of the President—is constitutional. Although the Supreme Court has no power to enforce its decisions, in our generation we have witnessed two events of historical importance when Presidents of the United States accepted and abided by the decisions of the Courts although they felt that they had acted within the scope of executive privilege and gave different interpretations of the Constitution than the Court did. In 1951, President Truman, who had seized the nation's steel mills in face of a nationwide strike, obeyed the Court's decision in the case of *Youngstown Street and Tube Co. v. Sawyer*, which declared the seizure unconstitutional. In 1974 President Nixon complied with the Court's decision ordering him to turn over tapes and documents related to the Watergate affair, which led to his resignation.

The Constitution designed a splendid model of a government with checks and balances. The doctrine of judicial review translated this vision into a legal reality. The judiciary is the safeguard of our constitutional rights. As Justice Charles Evans Hughes once stated: "We are under a Constitution, but the Constitution is what the judges say it is . . ." In the 200 years of history of our nation there has been no challenge on the part of the executive or legislative branches of our government to limit judicial power as the final arbiter on the question of which of our rights should be constitutionally protected.

Judge Patrick E. Higginbotham, in his lecture "Complexity's Challenge to Federalism: A Bicentennial Look to the Future," takes up the issue of divided

power even among the elements of the judiciary. One
of the unique aspects of the American system of jurisprudence is the independent legal system of each of
the fifty states—all with distinct powers and codes of
law. The federal judiciary system, of course, also has
authority over certain matters in each of these states.
In recent years, the lines demarcating jurisdiction
between these systems of state and federal courts
have become increasingly complex. With the vastly
increased quantities of litigation and the increased
mobility of our society, cases that involve a conflict of
jurisdiction between states have become much more
frequent as well.

Judge Higginbotham expresses concern that when
there is a conflict of applicable laws in different juris-
dictions, or when a large number of similar cases are
being tried as class actions in different states, there is
a growing tendency to develop and fall back on a
federal common law to deal with the disputes. He
believes that the system of divided power built into
our Constitution is a most valuable one, and that it
will take resourcefulness to find ways to streamline
justice without violating this system of checks and
balances, especially as they are embodied in the
various laws and legal systems of the fifty states. He
encourages us to keep in mind the vision of our
Founding Fathers in seeking to address this problem.

There are other ancient and abiding values long
cherished in our democracy that seem in danger of
falling by the wayside in view of recent judicial
decisions. The concept of the sovereign equality of all
men and of the dignity of every human being—as we
have seen, a product of Judaeo-Christian tradi-

tion—forms the foundation of our system of unalienable individual rights, which are not limited to
the "life, liberty, or property" listed in the
Fourteenth Amendment. Justice John Marshall
Harlan, commenting on the Fourteenth Amendment,
pointed out that "the intention of the people of the
United States was to prevent the deprivation of *any
legal right* in violation of the fundamental guarantees
inhering in due process of law [Emphasis added.]"
(*Taylor v. Beckham*, 178 U.S. 548, 599, 20 S.Ct. 890,
1014 [1899].) The legal rights of a person include his
right to the protection of his own reputation from
destructive attack and unjustified invasion.

In his lecture "Defamation: A Tale of Two Countries," Mr. George A. Birrell examines the history of
the law of defamation and libel in this country—the
set of laws designed to protect personal and corporate
reputation. He expresses alarm over what he sees as a
growing reluctance on the part of American
courts—under the leadership of the Supreme
Court—to protect people against defamation and libel
by awarding judgments against offenders. The courts
have changed standards in these matters so much
over recent decades that in many cases it has become
impossible for individuals—especially individuals in
public life—to achieve any sort of redress at all, no
matter how grievous the wrongs against them.

Mr. Birrell compares the development of American
law on these issues with English law. In several cases,
English committees, legislative bodies, and courts
have considered adopting or modeling their decisions
on American innovations in this area of the law, only
to deliberately reject such proposals to limit the

avenues of recourse for those who have been defamed
or libeled. Mr. Birrell expresses the view that
American courts and legislatures would do well to
return to the standards upheld in this country in the
past, which he believes better protected the rights of
American citizens.

Among other legal rights protected by the
guarantees inherent in the principle of due process of
law is the right to dissent. This country was founded
by dissenters. The right to dissent, the sacred right of
an individual to differ in his opinion from others, is in
our national bloodstream. This right, which is the
essence of tolerance, is in line with the basic concept
of democracy and the sovereign equality of all men.

In my lecture on "Tolerance," I tried to point out
the distinctive sources of political and religious
tolerance in the United States and why it is not
absolute at all times and under all circumstances.
Tolerance of intolerance, for instance, aggravates intolerance, while intolerance of intolerance safeguards
tolerance.

In the perspective of the tragedies the world has experienced under the oppression of totalitarian
regimes—which came to power through the abuse of
the tolerance offered by democracies—I maintain that
a balance should be sought between tolerance and the
primary and essential right to preserve our
democratic system. The freedoms of speech, of the
press, and of assembly exist under the law and not independently of it. The abuse of these freedoms tending to corrupt public morals or to incite rioting, looting, burning, or other crimes—abuses that present
threats to peace and public safety—must be punished

by a democratic state through the use of its police power.

This power, however, cannot be invoked in bad faith, as a cover for suppression or censorship. Free discussion cannot be denied, and the right of criticism cannot be stifled. The holders of power must always remain accountable for their actions. Our independent courts have been vested with the responsibility to protect the individual against capricious actions of the government and against any unreasonable encroachment upon the rights of the individual, as stipulated in the Constitution and the Bill of Rights.

In the 1987 Lectures on Moral Values in a Free Society, the theme is repeatedly emphasized that democracy is not a dogma limited to a certain place and time. Throughout recent history, we have witnessed the ascent and eventual fall of many dogmas that tried to offer a vision of a perfect society. In order not to suffer the fate of these passing dogmas, each generation, through its judges and duly elected representatives, has to breath new life into democracy—this forceful principle of political action capable of adjusting itself to the changes that constantly occur in any society. The strength of democracy lies in the ability to rise to challenges brought by the technological revolution, by social changes, and by other advances—to meet these dynamic components of historical change with appropriate evolutionary adjustments.

THE INTERACTION OF BUSINESS AND DEMOCRACY IN OUR POLITICAL SYSTEM

by

Charles B. Renfrew

Charles B. Renfrew

Charles B. Renfrew is Director and Vice-President, Law, of Chevron Corporation. He was previously a partner in the San Francisco law firm Pillsbury, Madison & Sutro, and served as United States District Judge for the Northern District of California from 1972 to 1980 and as Deputy Attorney General of the United States from 1980 to 1981.

Mr. Renfrew received his A.B. from Princeton University and his J.D. from the University of Michigan Law School. While serving on the bench, he taught part-time at the Boalt Hall School of Law at the University of California at Berkeley. He served in the U.S. Navy 1946-48 and as a First Lieutenant in the U.S. Army 1952-53.

Mr. Renfrew has served the American Bar Association as Vice-Chairman of its Antitrust Section, the San Francisco Lawyers Committee for Urban Affairs as co-chairman, and the Special Committee to Study the Problems of Discovery of the Federal Judicial Center as chairman. He was the Head of the United States Delegation to the Sixth United Nations Congress on the Prevention of Crime and the Treatment of Offenders held in Caracas, Venezuela, in 1980. He is a Research Fellow of The Southwestern Legal Foundation and a member of the Advisory Board of the Foundation's International and Comparative Law Center. He is a member of the American Law Institute, the American College of Trial Lawyers, and the American Judicature Society and a Fellow of the American Bar Foundation.

Among many other civic responsibilities, Mr. Renfrew serves on the Board of Directors of the National Judicial College, the American Petroleum Institute, the National Crime Prevention Council. He is Chairman of the Committee of the Bar of the NAACP Legal Defense and Educational Fund, Inc. He is on the National Lawyer Council of the Democratic National Committee, and formerly served as Alumni Trustee of Princeton University, as Chairman of the Diocesan Convention of the Episcopal Diocese of California, and as President of the Council for Civic Unity.

THE INTERACTION OF BUSINESS AND DEMOCRACY IN OUR POLITICAL SYSTEM

by

Charles B. Renfrew

Introduction

Before addressing the topic Dr. Cecil assigned me, "The Interaction of Business and Democracy in Our Political System," I should explain that I have used capitalism, or the market–driven economy, as synonymous with business in the United States. In this paper, I shall trace the development of capitalistic and democratic values and traditions in the United States, examine their interdependency, look at some of the tensions or conflicts between them, try to explain why capitalism is often maligned while democracy is universally revered, point out why socialism is not a viable alternative to capitalism—neither as an economic system nor as a basis for a democratic society—and finally I will offer a few suggestions as to how we might best preserve and accommodate the values of capitalism and democracy, the principal components of the American political system. Their preservation is essential because it is my thesis that democracy can only flourish in a market-driven economy. I will even go further—such an economy inevitably leads to democracy. (My thesis is neither original nor profound but it is significant, and public

awareness and understanding of it is vital to the
preservation of our political system. For those interested in pursuing this topic in greater depth, I highly
recommend two books which I found extremely in-
formative and most helpful in preparing this paper:
Michael Novak's *Spirit of Democratic Capitalism*,
Simon & Schuster, 1982; and *The American Ethos:
Public Attitudes Toward Capitalism and Democracy*,
Herbert McClosky and John Zaller, A Twentieth
Century Fund Report, Harvard University Press,
1984.)

Historical Development of Democracy and Capitalism

Let me begin, if I may, by asking you to go back
with me to the middle of the eighteenth century to
look at the world as it existed at that time. There was
no separation or distinction between the economic
and the political systems. All power resided in an
authoritarian government, whether a Czar, an
Emperor, King, or Pasha, it mattered little. As the
iron grip of feudalism had loosened, people had
migrated to towns and cities. In the cities, men were
freer. They worked under the collective benefit of
guilds or other organizations of men pursuing the
same occupation. Economic advantage, however, was
a matter of privilege. Licenses and grants from the
ruler to a special few were the order of the day. This
was the era of mercantilism. Basically, one's situation
in life was determined at birth. There were traditional
restraints imposed by the aristocracy, the Church,
and the privileged. Effort or ability had little impact

or change upon one's station. Whenever slight gains were enjoyed, they were subjected to crippling taxes, and life was controlled by traditional restraints, rules, and regulations.

Most of the world was unmapped. Poverty was widespread. Elementary hygiene was unknown. Illiteracy was almost universal. Very few cities had plumbing systems. Potable water was rarely available. Thus the world had been, and so it appeared it would always be.

In such a world, as Michael Novak, the conservative Catholic philosopher, has pointed out:

> "Famines ravaged the civilized world on the average once a generation. Plagues seized scores of thousands. In the 1780's, four-fifths of French families devoted 90 percent of their incomes simply to buying bread—only bread—to stay alive. Life expectancy in 1795 in France was 27.3 years for women and 23.4 for men. In the year 1800, in the whole of Germany fewer than a thousand people had incomes as high at $1,000." (Michael Novak, *Spirit of Democratic Capitalism*, Simon & Schuster, 1982, p. 16)

There was, however, a growing ray of hope in this bleak and desperate world, for this was also the age of enlightenment. As men wrote of the human situation, they speculated as to how the world might be made a better place. Change was in the air.

It was in this world and at that time that two isolated events occurred—each in 1776—which I have selected as marking the commencement of our democratic and capitalistic traditions and values. They are, of course, the signing of the Declaration of Independence and the publishing of Adam Smith's *An Inquiry into the Nature and Cause of the Wealth of Nations*. Interestingly enough, it was also in 1776 that another Scot, James Watt, began the manufacture of his improved steam engine, which played a significant role in the industrial revolution that followed.

The Declaration of Independence was followed by the Articles of Confederation, the Federalist papers, and finally the Constitution and its Bill of Rights, a document whose Bicentennial we celebrate this year and whose vitality and significance has never been greater. William Gladstone, an English Prime Minister, once referred to our Constitution as "the most wondrous work ever struck by the mind and purpose of man." We must remember, however, that while the Constitution is a "living document," to be so, it must live in the minds and hearts of Americans if we are to pass it on to successive generations.

From these sources sprang the democratic values of our society. Similarly the free-market teachings of Adam Smith underlie the economic system and its values which ultimately took root in America. These two values constitute the American dream as well as its creed.

We are all familiar with the values underlying democracy and capitalism as they have evolved. In a democracy, all people are equal and have the right to participate in government either directly or by their duly elected representatives. The elected, in turn, are responsible to the electorate. They must observe "due process" in their governance. While the majority rules, minority rights must be respected. Both the governed and those who govern are equal before the law and have the same essential rights. These rights are set forth in our Constitution and include freedom of speech, press, assembly, and religion.

Under capitalism, through private ownership of the means of production and distribution, self-interested individuals seek profit through their efforts. It requires a free competitive market operating according to the laws of supply and demand. Such a market determines which goods and services are produced or made available, the price at which they are sold, the profits earned on their sale, and the wages paid to workers. There is also the corollary belief in the so-called Protestant ethic, with its emphasis upon achievement and hard work.

Our political system not only reflects the values of capitalism and democracy, it does not exist apart from them.

Adam Smith believed that economic development or wealth could be created through the application of man's intelligence. That concept—that improvement in one's economic condition was possible—was unique at that time but fell on fertile soil in America. In 1776, almost all believed that governmental control of planning from the top was more orderly and more effective. Smith saw that an economic system works best when it works from the bottom up, not from the top down. In that way, it calls upon the collective talent of every individual, not merely the abilities of a few. Like our political forefathers, he had a profound trust in individual rationality. While there were occasions when the body politic had to interfere with the market—and this could be useful and commendable, basically the market best served the common good when freed from governmental restraint.

The economic system envisioned by Smith would free the intelligence, imagination, and industry of individuals from restraint and enlist them through enlightened self-interest to help create a better world. For Smith saw that the new order would not only benefit Scotland and Great Britain but the entire world. He predicted that in such a world it would be possible through the exercise of rational self-interest to abolish famines and raise material standards. Thus, far from a narrow or selfish perspective, capitalism has as its ultimate goal economic development for all nations. When the economies of Japan and Western Europe were destroyed in World War II, it was not just our democratic traditions that led the United States to assist in their recovery, it was also pursuant to a basic tenet of capitalism. The amazing success of those efforts was also dramatic evidence of the strength of capitalism.

Smith saw that a voluntary market transaction would not take place unless both sides thought they would benefit from it. Smith further saw the market not as statistical sums or averages but rather as a series of individual transactions by individual buyers and sellers. Even today, too many in government think of stimulating the economy rather than stimulating individuals. The latter requires a knowledge of personal concerns, goals, and incentives. Statistics follow—not lead—the acts of individuals in the market. As Smith pointed out, "[I]t is not from the benevolence of the butcher, the brewer, or the baker that we expect our dinner, but from their regard to their own interest." The concept of trusting individual judgments in the marketplace reinforces our confidence in the ordinary wisdom of citizens as voters or jurors and in carrying out their daily lives.

While Smith advocated self-reliance, he did not stop there. He pointed out that every self is both individual and social and has both selfish and benevolent interests. He wrote, regarding the latter, "[T]o feel much for others, and little for ourselves, that to restrain our selfish, and to indulge our benevolent affections constitute the perfection of human nature." While Smith advocated self-reliance, he did not stop there. Above all, there was the need for playing by the rules. Individual action had to conform to the standards or mores of the greater society.

> "In the race for wealth, and honours, and preferments, he may run as hard as he can, and strain every nerve and every muscle, in order to outstrip all his competitiors. But if he should jostle or throw down any of them, the indulgence of the spectators is entirely at an end. It is a violation of fair play, which they cannot admit of."

To Smith, it was the social outcome of an economic order that was crucial, not the personal intentions of the individuals who comprised it. We all know good intentions do not necessarily create good results.

Smith took this simple axiom and applied it to the economic order. We must look to the results and judge the system by those results.

By 1800, popular self-government was rare. Great Britain and the United States were among the few democracies. Our Founding Fathers were proud of what they had done. That pride and their lofty ambition are reflected on the back of the basic unit of our currency—the one-dollar bill. There are two Latin phrases which should be noted. The first, on the right-hand side, is on the scroll in the beak of the eagle, the American bird. It reads "E PLURIBUS UNUM"—or one from many. Those who helped create our republic knew they had a population which was diverse and came from many sources. Yet, they expected a single unifying commitment to the values and traditions of our democracy, which are contained in the Constitution. The second phrase is under an unfinished pyramid, which is beneath the eye of God. The phrase is "NOVUS ORDO SECLORUM," or a new order of the ages. The pyramid was selected because it symbolized both strength and antiquity. It was unfinished because our democracy—and our economy, I might add—are always in the building. And build we did.

Alexis de Tocqueville came to America from France and looked and listened and above all observed. His *Democracy in America*, first published in 1835, was his insightful analysis of American political, economic, and social institutions. It is considered by scholars to be not only "the greatest book ever written on America, but probably the greatest on any national polity and culture."

De Tocqueville, watching the building of this new order of the ages, noted that everywhere in America, people were "calculating and weighing and compiling." He commented that there was an unleashing of raw energy in the activities of the mechanics and artisans, farmers and carpenters, men and women of every station who felt they could make their own world. A factor contributing to this activity was that each member of a family had the same opportunities. The American laws of inheritance did not follow the European principle of primogeniture. This prevented the retention of large estates and led to increased commercial activity and industry.

The Interdependency of Democracy and Capitalism

The close relationship between our economic and democratic systems is not simply an accident of history. Both sprang from a common background. Each was a reaction or protest against society as it then existed. Each sought to limit the power of the state. Each sought to protect the individual and harness his energies and talents. Each sought to break the traditional restraints which permitted the exploitation of the less fortunate by the privileged. Their common origin explains why these two systems share so many of the same values—a commitment to freedom and individualism; limited government; equality before the law; a belief in the rights of property; the value of open competition; decision-making based upon rationality, not by the feudal or authoritarian basis which had dominated before; and a belief in our Constitution and the basic rights it protects.

The extraordinary emphasis on freedom in the American political system also reinforces the capitalistic economic system. The greater the emphasis on individual freedom, the more likely that the individual will be free to compete economically, that one may choose his or her vocation and determine which goods and services to produce and sell. Capitalism is based upon such freedom, and, to the extent that it results in a stronger economic system, the political system itself is reinforced.

The broad-based societal support for capitalism and democracy created our political culture, and the characteristic elements of those traditions establish the possible limits of political change. Take, for example, the political protests of the 1960s. Only those protests which were compatible with the traditional American values were successful. Public control of large corporations failed because of the tradition of private property—a basic tenet of capitalism. Political protests, such as urban guerrilla tactics, were not successful because they conflicted with the democratic principles of free elections, peaceful debate, and orderly and responsible opposition. Where the protests were consistent with the American creed, they were successful and extended traditional values to new groups and in new situations: greater equality for minorities and women; political dissent against participation in the Viet Nam War; and greater personal freedoms, e.g., abortion, the rights of homosexuals, and so on.

As democracy and capitalism have evolved, they have become interdependent. One cannot survive without the other. A society in which there exists a market-driven economy or capitalism without political liberties is inherently unstable. In the market-driven economy, the individual has the freedom of choice, the ability to express himself or herself by selection as to occupation, what to produce, how to get it to the marketplace, and at what price to sell or buy it. These freedoms, the ability to participate in the decisionmaking that is the free market, causes individuals with those freedoms to ask—to demand—comparable rights in the political system. Citizens who are economically free to pursue their own interests ultimately will demand the political freedom to do the same in that sphere.

South Korea is a classic example of two truths. The first is that an economic system in which individual participants are rewarded for their efforts, one which works from the bottom up, not imposed from the top down, is the most productive. The second is that democracy, unless precluded by external forces, inevitably will follow a market-driven economy. Conventional wisdom following World War II, based upon Keynesian economics, taught that the newly emerging countries in the Third World, even if democratic, needed to have a state-run economy in order to raise their economic status to a so-called "take-off" level, after which a more open economic system might be viable. Unfortunately, none of those state-imposed economies ever got to the "take-off" level. South Korea has been a textbook classic in this respect.

Following the devastation of the Korean War, the Korean economy has had a fantastic growth. While there has been a strong government influence, it has followed a market-driven route. Today the South Koreans, who have seen their country developed at a dazzling rate and have voted in the market as to their preferences, are now demanding participation in the political system as well. The result, barring external intervention, is inescapable. They will participate, and the authoritarian hold will crack.

John Kenneth Galbraith in a recent article in *The New York Times* said that economic and industrial development inevitably leads to democracy. He sees economic development as the vital engine of democracy. While he does not speak in terms of a capitalist economy, he does refer to an economy in which a large number of people, individually and in organizations, insist on participating. These are not practices consistent with the socialist model. Indeed, he points out:

> "There is no advanced industrial country outside the socialistic world that does not have in one form or another, a democratically oriented government."

And so it is in the United States and Canada, Japan, Australia, New Zealand, India (now an emerging industrial power), Brazil, Argentina, Mexico, Israel, and all of Western Europe. While some cite Sweden, Israel, and West Germany as democratic states which are also socialistic, each one of them has large and significant components of private property and extensive use of private markets. There are also private incentives and awards which flow to those who succeed in those markets.

Galbriath points out that the opposite occurs in the nonindustrial world; there, democracy is the exception.

> "Here there is the military dictatorship, the civilian strongarm or a permanently dominant minority. What in the industrially developed world is the rule is in the nonindustrial world sadly the exception to the rule."

The growing list of countries which have recently become industrialized and developed and which have demanded the rights of self-expression and democratic participation in the political system include Spain, Greece, Argentina, Brazil, other countries in Latin America, and most recently the Philippines and South Korea, as we have noted.

Based upon these examples and experiences, it follows that so someday will follow Taiwan, Chile, Pakistan, Indonesia, eventually South Africa, and finally the Arab world. We are beginning to see cracks today even in the Socialist world. Where there are parts of the economy in those societies that are market-driven, where people participate in economic decisionmaking to that extent, then that desire to participate, to express one's self, is felt elsewhere in the system. Events in Czechoslovakia, Hungary, and Poland confirm this observation. It is interesting to speculate what ultimately might have occurred in those countries in the absence of the brooding omnipresence of the Soviet Army. Today we see in even the Soviet Union and China some opening, some relaxing of the iron grip, some concession to the demands of their own people to be heard.

For too long, we in the West have secretly been fearful that perhaps Marx was correct as to the inevitability of the triumph of Communism. History has proved his economic theories to be fatally flawed and his predictions to be wrong. We now know there is an unseen but vital link between capitalism and democracy.

Tensions and Conflicts Within the Capitalistic and Democratic Values and Between Them

Not all the values associated with capitalism and democracy are mutually consistent. There are tensions, even conflicts, as there must be in any complex society. There are situations in which popular sovereignty and the rights of individuals are not always harmonious. While the majority must govern, it must do so with due respect to the rights of the minority. The Founding Fathers were well aware that such conflicts would arise, and they created a system of checks and balances to avoid a tyranny of the majority. They were concerned about the concentration of power in a single source. No one was good enough or wise enough to have such power. Thus, institutions such as church, state, press, and economic institutions, among others, were separated from the state. Since society consisted of so many factions, obtaining a majority required accommodation to different interests. Coalitions would change and shift, depending upon the issue to be determined. This diffusion of power was felt to be a means of protecting against an all-powerful majority. The respect for the minority and the need to obtain coalition consensus is part of a tradition, yet reflects values in conflict.

Perhaps the highest value in the American creed is freedom. As Clinton Rossiter once said:

> "We have always been a nation obsessed with liberty. Liberty over authority, freedom over responsibility, rights over duties—these are our historic preferences. From the days of Williams and Wise to those of Eisenhower and Kennedy, Americans have talked about practically nothing else but liberty. Not the good man, but the free man has been the measure of all things in this 'sweet land of liberty;' not national glory but individual liberty has been the object of political authority and the test of its worth."

While no society can be absolutely free, it is undisputed that our freedom of religion, speech, press, assembly, and individual freedoms with respect to morals have all been increasing for a number of reasons. In such a society, there is bound to be a profound tension between the forces of social cohesion and the ideal of unrestrained freedom.

Perhaps the most dramatic and the starkest conflict involves what I perceive to be the second highest value in our society, that of equality—the concept that all individuals have inherently the same worth with the same dignity. De Tocqueville found the American society he visited dominated by a "passion for equality."

> "No novelty in the United States struck me more vividly during my stay there than the equality of condition. It was easy to see the immense influence of this basic fact in the course of society. It gives a particular turn to public opinion, and a particular twist to the laws, new maxims to those who govern and particularly habits to the governed."

This observation holds true today.

De Tocqueville felt that men in a democratic state have an "instinctive taste for freedom," but it was equality "for which they feel an eternal love." He cautioned that this passion had a negative as well as a positive side.

> "[The] passion for equality . . . rouses in all men a desire to be strong and respected. This passion tends to elevate the little man to the ranks of the great. But the human heart also nourishes a debased taste for equality, which leads the weak to want to drag the strong to their level and which induces men to prefer equality in servitude to inequality in freedom."

The tradition of equality is most difficult and elusive to precisely define as it continues to evolve in different arenas, political, legal, moral, and economic. The subject of the meaning of equal opportunity, which has evolved to include affirmative action in today's world, inspires much debate and would require additional lectures.

The most basic conflict in values comes between the values associated with freedom and individualism and those of equality. Those who have the greater talent and skills, work harder, or take greater risks are entitled to keep the gains they receive by reason of those characteristics. Since individuals have widely differing skills and talents, there are bound to be widely differing economic gains resulting from the application of their efforts in a competitive society, and, as we know, inequality of wealth often leads to inequality of opportunity. Yet how does this reconcile with the concept of equality? Not easily. Arthur Okun, an economist and former chairman of President Johnson's Council of Economic Advisors, stated:

> "American society proclaims the worth of every human being. All citizens are guaranteed equal justice and equal rights. . . . As American citizens, we are the members of the same club.
>
> "Yet at the same time, our institutions say, 'find a job or go hungry,' 'succeed or suffer.' They prod us to get ahead of our neighbors economically after telling us to stay in line socially. They award prizes that allow the big winners to feed their pets better than the losers can feed their children.
>
> "Such is the double standard of a capitalist democracy, professing and pursuing an equalitarian political and social system and simultaneously generating gaping disparities in economic wellbeing."

Not all agree with this position. A recent poll cited 87 percent of the "opinion leaders" (politically active or influential respondents) asserted "our freedom depends on the free enterprise system." Milton Friedman argues forcibly that if government can ever abolish the right to own property, to manufacture and sell goods in the free market, and to determine the course of one's own economic life, citizens would become so dependent upon the state for their livelihood that they would soon lose their democratic right to self-government as well.

Before leaving the subject of conflicts with our values, I would like to mention briefly the most serious conflict between our democratic values and our practices, which has involved the treatment of blacks in America. This is the most grievous and certainly the most sordid of our failures to live up to the American creed. De Tocqueville warned thirty years before the Civil War: "The most formidable evil threatening the future of the United States is the presence of the blacks on their soil." He noted, "No African came in freedom to the shores of the New World." Since the slave was from another race, he differed "from his master not only in lacking freedom but also in his origin. You can make the Negro free, but you cannot prevent him facing the European as a stranger."

The existence of our ideals, however, has played an important role. That a gulf exists between one's ideals and one's practice is not necessarily totally negative. The presence of the ideal may create discomfort and guilt. Surely it did so for many whites, since they knew that their treatment of blacks was contrary to their basic democratic values. It may have made at least some more willing to work for reform. This was the conclusion of Gunnar Myrdal in his seminal study of black-white relations in America. He stated that concerned whites who knew that the treatment of blacks in this country was indefensible were the strongest supporters for reform.

While great strides have been made, much remains to be done. As de Tocqueville predicted, "When they have abolished slavery, the masters still have to eradicate three much more intangible and tenacious prejudices: the prejudice of the master, the prejudice of race, and the prejudice of the white." I hope we heed his words and continue the building of the new order of the ages as our forefathers contemplated.

The Distrust and Dislike of Capitalism

In light of the perceived conflict between the values of equality with certain of the values of individualism or freedom, many "caring" people find the economic disparities referred to by Arthur Okun objectionable. They wonder whether a country which upholds the ideals of political equality and equal opportunity, on the one hand, can have economic inequality, on the other hand. Even though capitalism as an economic system is not universal throughout the world, as a target for hatred it is. The word evokes hatred in socialist countries; and, even domestically, people associate it with selfishness, exploitation, and inequity. A recent public debate about capitalism was reported in *Harper's Magazine* (Dec. 1986). The opening sentence read: "Capitalism, like original sin, is one of the primary dogmas that nobody likes to defend."

In the debate which followed, it was clear that at least two of the participants had great scorn and derision for capitalism as an economic system which underscores democratic values. In that debate and many others where capitalism is attacked, people fail to distinguish between wealth and capital. The capitalist economy produces a profit which creates wealth, but it depends upon it—or some of it—being used as capital. Wealth may be hoarded or used for consumption and be nonproductive. Capital, on the other hand, is that part of wealth which is reinvested in productive activities. Perhaps capital should be referred to as economic development. If one does away with profits, then one stops the production of new wealth which in turn would preclude further economic development.

It is of interest, as Joseph Schumpeter pointed out more than forty-five years ago, that many intellectuals are opposed to capitalism. They deplore the very concept of the marketplace as the determiner of rewards. However, they, without exception, enthusiastically support the concept of a free marketplace in ideas—an endorsement, I suppose, of the values articulated in John Milton's *Areopagitica*. Yet the same considerations apply. In each market, no one person shall tell others what to buy or which ideas to accept; in each market, thousands of individual transactions determine the acceptability of an idea or a product.

However, it is obvious that not all the criticisms of capitalism and some of its excesses are without basis. We do need to concern ourselves with the needs of the disadvantaged, to deal with the poor and the hungry. The lure of socialism is that it directly confronts these needs and guarantees a solution. But no matter how much the Socialist dream captures the imagination of some well-intended minds, in practice it fails. The simple truth remains. No matter what the worthy intentions of the socialist dreamers, the society they create in the long run will increase poverty and legitimize tyranny. The record of almost all the sub-Sahara African states stands as tragic witness to this fact.

Furthermore, it must be kept in mind that capitalism, as it has evolved, is not static. It is dynamic and is always growing and changing. Our democratic traditions do permit popular majorities to impose upon market determination when necessary to alleviate social and economic distress. The New Deal legislation in the 1930s and the Civil Rights Acts and Great Society legislation of the 1960s are examples. The disadvantaged in the United States are helped through a variety of programs. The key here is the extent of interference with the mechanism of the market. The less interference, the better, and where it is determined to interfere, the interference should be undertaken with an awareness of its purpose and its consequence upon the market. We must not lose sight of the fundamental fact that the market is essential to the survival of our republic.

Let me address one particular current criticism.

There is a great deal of public clamor and discussion about increasing materialism—leading to moral disarray. Felix G. Rohatyn, an investment banker and public citizen, charges:

> "Greed and corruption are the cancer of a free society. They are a cancer because they erode our value system. They create contempt for many of our institutions as a result of the corrupt actions of individuals."

He is right, but that is not a condemnation of capitalism, because corruption is totally inconsistent with and contrary to a free market. And unrestricted greed for oneself is not part of capitalism nor consistent with its spirit.

Much of the fault seems to be directed toward those involved with our financial institutions and markets. Much of the blame is doubtlessly deserved. The Ivan Boeskys of the world must be punished, for they have broken the law and by their misappropriation of insider information have threatened the integrity of our financial markets. But we must go slowly with reform. As a British politician once said during a crisis, "Reform, don't talk to me of reform; we are in enough trouble as it is."

We must not let concern with insider trading scandals be used as a lever to enact antitakeover legislation which may cause more problems that it attempts to cure. Such legislation can entrench incumbent management and reward inefficiency. While we need to deal with insiders, we should do so directly and make sure we protect the integrity of our markets—not existing management. Antitakeover legislation would also deprive stockholders of legitimate profits. To do so because some insiders also have made profits is comparable to closing banks because there have been bank robberies.

We also need to be careful about diagnosing a cure for so-called "junk bonds." The market has already done so. Their risk premium already covered the default rate for such bonds in 1985 and 1986. While we are told institutional investors have changed the market irreversibly by just looking at the next quarter's earnings, we do know that the market can take a longer view, hence the large prices for stock of biotechnology and other high-tech companies. Again, it is the market's integrity we must protect and preserve.

A totally regulated and controlled economy and financial markets with excessive rules is not the answer. That environment breeds inefficiency and stifles the creativity and energy we need.

Boesky and Levin were caught by our self-regulating mechanisms and our regulatory system. We have had tremendous growth and prosperity following the enactment of the securities legislation of 1933 and 1934. While we need to deal with the problems caused by the unfettered greed and corruption that our news media depict daily, we should do so as precisely as possible, weighing the consequences intended or otherwise of such legislation and regulation, bearing always in mind that we must protect the integrity of our financial markets without interfering with the free flow of information to the marketplace.

Socialism Is Not a Viable Alternative if One Wishes to Preserve Democratic Values

As recently as a half century ago, Paul Tillich, a leading theologian, was taken seriously when he asserted that any serious Christian must be a socialist. Even today, a number of Catholic priests find intellectual attraction to Marxism. Father Arthur McGovern, S.J., explains thusly:

> "Many Christians are deeply troubled by conditions in the world, by the vast gap between wealthy, affluent people and disparately poor ones, by vast expenditure on military weapons and luxury goals while basic human needs go unmet, by the growing power of great corporations, and by a culture which undermines Christian values and true human needs."

One could look at Marxist states and have the same concerns. However, as a practical matter, socialism is no longer an alternative for a society which wishes to retain its democratic traditions.

Daniel Bell has declared, "The most unreported of our era is the death of socialism." There are those who dispute the essential link between capitalism and democracy, but the countries they point to as examples of socialism in a democratic state—Sweden, Israel, and West Germany—each contain large components of private property, markets, and incentives. Because of its failures in the economic sphere, socialism has been forced to retreat to the political arena. Thus, while socialism has spread to the Third World, notably in South America and

Southern Africa, this has not occurred in a democratic environment.

As Michael Novak has pointed out:

"Nationalized industries do not prevent low wages to workers, do not conspicuously improve working conditions, do not diminish environmental damage and do not raise levels of efficiency, material progress, and humane attitudes in the work force."

Where portions of agricultural land remain in private hands in socialist regimes such as Hungary and China, they have outperformed collectivized state agriculture by factors as high as 30-to-1, despite far higher concentrations of resources (machinery, fertilizer, rock, etc.) devoted to state collectives.

Again, administered prices and wages have been shown to be less intelligent, efficient, and rational than those determined by the free-market mechanism.

Interestingly, even the Marxists now acknowledge the economic failure of socialism. The most recent denouncement of the socialist economic model comes from Jose Eduardo dos Santos, the President of Angola and an avowed Marxist, who blamed his country's poor economic condition on excessive socialist planning and Government bureaucracy. He said practices have fostered "disorganization, poor entrepreneurial management, and rampant indiscipline and corruption." President dos Santos has sought to decentralize economic planning and to encourage private enterprise. He "has underscored the need to open and encourage private initiatives in many areas, including retail trade, transportation, construction, farming, cattle raising and elsewhere throughout the service sector." (*The New York Times*, August 26, 1987.)

As an economic theory, socialism does not work in practice, but it is a formidable political institution. The classless society envisioned by Marx is nonexistent. Its promise has turned to ashes. In reality, because of the concentration of power in the state, the so-called classless society is but another name for terror. As a French commentator pointed out:

> "the Gulag is not a blunder or an accident, not a simple wound or aftereffect of Stalinsim; but the necessary corollary of a socialism which can only actualize homogeneity back to its fringes, which can aim for the universal only by confirming its rebels, its irreducible individualists, in the outer darkness of a nonsociety. . . . No socialism without camps, *no classless society without its terrorist truth.*" (Levy, *Barbarism with a Human Face*, Tr. George Holock, Harper & Row, 1979, p. 158.)

The recent and unparalleled self-genocide of Cambodia could have only occurred in a socialist-classless state.

Preservation and Accommodation of the Values of Capitalism and Democracy

In correcting excesses of capitalism to accommodate our traditional values of democracy, we have rejected radical or extreme solutions. There can be no "final solution," because, as the one-dollar bill tells us, our republic will always be building, always in a state of change. Whatever changes are made must be based upon our traditional values.

Dr. James O'Toole, professor of management at the University of Southern California, suggests that our economic system can balance and take into account all the conflicting demands made upon it, by providing justice as one of the key concepts in our democratic tradition, which will not require any of the demands to be ignored. The matrix of demands he sees are the four "great themes" of contemporary political life: liberty, equality, efficiency, and the quality of life. These are, he believes, the polar forces affecting our economy.

Those who espouse liberty as the highest value advocate policies which reduce the role of government and emphasize the role and significance of the individual.

Those who see equality as the highest goal see unjust disparities in income and power resulting from market distribution and seek to increase the role of the government.

Efficiency is the highest goal of those who seek economic development and growth. While I believe economic development follows directly from policies which support the market-driven economy, Professor O'Toole believes that growth will result from the development of national economic policies, which involve building cooperative arrangements between business, government, and labor.

Finally, those who favor quality of life are the

humanist/environmentalists who wish to stop con-
spicuous consumption, conserve national resources,
and reduce pollution and who believe "small is
beautiful." Some even support anti- or no-growth
policies.

O'Toole suggests that the legitimate concern of
each of these groups can be met by the following
modifications or accommodations within the capitalistic economic system:

(1) Individualistic concerns are met by corporations
engaging in enlightened self-regulation. For example,
by voluntarily taking into account the needs of all
participants in the economic system, the necessity to
appeal to the government to intervene in the marketplace and thus in the private affairs of corporations
and citizens is significantly reduced. By engaging in
voluntary philanthropic activities, and by addressing
society's major problems as business opportunities,
corporate America will reduce the scope, range, and,
thus, the coercive power of the government.

(2) Egalitarian concerns are met through employee
stock ownership and profit sharing. Worker capitalism
more effectively meets the problems of income dis-
parity than does state ownership and state redistribu-
tion—and does so without the drawbacks of
bureaucratic inefficiency. Corporate full-employment
strategies can reduce the effects of booms and busts
on employees.

(3) Concerns for growth, efficiency, and international competitiveness are met by corporate commitment to research and development, the fullest utilization of human resources, the latest technology, and
the most effective planning.

(4) Humanistic concerns are met by policies of decentralization, utilization of small work units, greater worker participation, and enhanced quality of work life programs. Environmentalist concerns are met by voluntary efforts to provide worker health and safety, consumer safety, and environmental protection, rather than awaiting and then complying with government regulation.

When asked some 200 years ago what occurred in Philadelphia, Benjamin Franklin was reported to have replied, "We have built a Republic, if you can keep it." What I have tried to point out is that during these past two centuries what we have done—more precisely—is engage in the building of a capitalistic republic. Keeping it is still the crucial issue. It is a system of amazing strength and resiliency that is capable of tremendous staying power. We do face serious external threats from the socialist world. To these challenges we need to be constantly on guard. Less obvious or apparent, however, and perhaps equally as dangerous is the internal threat we face. This internal threat comes about chiefly from our failure to recognize the vital linkage between our economic system and our democratic way of life. If we ignore this essential interdependency and subject our economic system to demands and controls which impair its ability to bring forth the collective talents and efforts of every individual, then the base upon which we are building our great Republic will become stagnant. That will have profound consequences upon our ability to continue our democratic way of life. Awareness of and acting in accord with the inextricably intertwined relationship between capitalism and democracy will ensure that our republic—as our forefathers had proudly proclaimed—will always be in the building.

SOME UNDERPINNINGS OF AMERICAN CONSTITUTIONAL DEMOCRACY

by

William Lee Miller

William Lee Miller

William Lee Miller is the Miller Center Professor of Ethics and Institutions at the White Burkett Miller Center of Public Affairs at the University of Virginia. He also serves as chairman of the Department of Rhetoric and Communication Studies, Professor of Rhetoric, and Professor of Religious Studies. Prior to joining the Virginia faculty in 1982, Professor Miller taught at Yale University, Smith College, and Indiana University, where he was the Director of the Poynter Center on American Institutions for ten years.

Professor Miller received his A.B. from the University of Nebraska and his B.D. and Ph.D. from Yale University. He was a staff writer and editor for The Reporter *magazine from 1955 to 1958 and has contributed many articles to scholarly journals, magazines, and anthologies. He is the author of* The Protestant and Politics *(1960),* Piety Along the Potomac *(1964),* The Fifteenth Ward and the Great Society *(1966),* Of Thee, Nevertheless, I Sing: An Essay on American Political Values *(1975),* Yankee from Georgia: The Emergence of Jimmy Carter *(1978), and* The First Liberty: Religion and the American Republic *(1986).*

In addition to participating in many other distinguished lectureships and receiving a number of study awards, Professor Miller has been an Annenberg Distinguished Scholar at the Center for the Study of the American Experience at the University of Southern California, a Guest Scholar at the Woodrow Wilson Center for International Scholars at the Smithsonian Institution, and a Visiting Scholar at the Kennedy Institute for Ethics at Georgetown University. He has directed seminars for journalists at Williams College for the National Endowment for the Humanities and moderated seminars at the Aspen Institute for Humanistic Studies.

Professor Miller has also served actively in public affairs, writing speeches for the Stevenson campaign in 1956, serving as an Alderman for the city of New Haven, and assisting Vice President Hubert Humphrey with his book Beyond Civil Rights. *He was a member of the Commission on International Justice and Goodwill of the National Council of Churches and a Trustee of the Church Peace Union Council on Religion and International Affairs.*

SOME UNDERPINNINGS OF
AMERICAN CONSTITUTIONAL DEMOCRACY

by

William Lee Miller

One: The Constitution Shuts the Door

There is perhaps no phrase associated with our American constitutional system more familiar to the ordinary citizen than this one: "checks and balances." During the summer of the constitution's bicentennial, that phrase got quite a workout—not only in the celebrations but also in current events. Worried legislators tried to explain its meaning to a bumptious marine colonel, and through television to his fans in the public. Advocates on one side and the other tussled over its meaning in Senate hearings on the allegedly unbalancing addition to a most important balancing institution, the Supreme Court. And the bicentennial celebration itself invoked that phrase again and again as it worked its way through the summer commemorating the one in which the Constitution was written.

Upon what theory does this "checks and balances" rest? The answer used to be: upon the realistic view of human nature held by that large portion of the original Americans whose religion was part of the Reformed tradition. In a book about the United States that once was said (a long time ago, to be sure) to be a part of the education of every American college graduate, *The American Commonwealth* by the sometime British ambassador, Lord Bryce, there is a passage that was often quoted, with hearty approval, in American sermons and speeches and books of a religious tendency. "There is," Bryce wrote, "a hearty Puritanism in the view of human nature that pervades the instrument of 1787. It is the work of men who believed in original sin, and were resolved to leave open no door which they could possibly shut."

And certainly the instrument composed in Philadelphia in the summer of 1787 does include a pattern of restraints that seems to rest upon reservations about human goodness.

There is the separation of powers in the central government, with the executive, legislative, and judicial "branches" separated and equal, but also intricately cross-related in reciprocal restraints: They can shut the door on each other.

So can the two houses of Congress, originally even more distinct than now. The Senate, smaller, with longer terms and unlimited debate, represented the *states*, equally, as a result of the compromise that made the Constitution possible; it was to provide a more deliberate and cautious body in which the passions of the popular body would be allowed to cool, as tea in a saucer. The House, on the other hand, the popular body, was to shut the door on the aristocratic tendencies of the Senate; it was given the decisive power of originating money bills.

There is the more original and remarkable institution of judicial review under which, at the top, nine judges appointed for life, the "least dangerous branch," with no army or purse strings, can shut the door on "unconstitutional" acts by all the others.

There is the Bill of Rights, the amendments that many of the new Americans insisted be attached to the new constitution, and which were attached in 1789-1791, providing a written guarantee of citizens' rights: It shuts the door against arbitrary government. Since the passage of the Fourteenth Amendment and its interpretation by the Court, it has done so not only against the federal but also against the state governments. It is, of course, because of this combination—judicial review and the federal guarantees applied against the states—that these original institutions have become so important a check to the others, and we have thus witnessed the fierce fight over a crucial addition to the Court.

The checkings and balancings are not simply within the national government. The federal system, dividing power between the states and the federal government, both acting directly upon the individual citizen in a way that theretofore has been thought impossible, provided further reciprocal door-shuttings against local and national tyrannies.

And the most important check of them all reaches outside these governments entirely to their source in the people's voting—in regular and frequent elections (the wary anti-Federalists wanted them to be even more frequent.) The makers of the laws at every level of American government must at regular intervals come back to face the electorate and give the people a chance to throw this particular set of rascals out and to put in a new set . . . a shutting of the door on unresponsive, arbitrary government.

The American political system, despite the intentions of the founders, went on to develop other institutions, the political party and the two-party system, which, although they have a kind of a base in the Constitution—in the single member district system, in the big prize of the Presidency, and in the protections of free agitation and assembling—were an accidental addition, which the founders did not want, but which many of us now regard as being desirable and in the spirit of the original institutions. In fact, we hope the plebiscitary politics of the television set does not wipe out the role of the parties.

It is very important to understand that this principle of limited, divided, balanced, and reciprocally checking power, *formally* instituted by Americans in our constitutional system, was a principle that applied not only to *government* but also to *society.* The balancing was informally represented in the pluralism of interests and social groups, performing the same service—a certain shutting of the door on each other—out in the interplay of politics and society that the formal institutions of the Constitution do in the workings of government. Madison himself, of course, made this perhaps the most famous point in *The Federalist*. He turned the argument of the anti–Federalists and the ancients on its head. They said republican government could exist only in small city-states, where face to face meeting was possible. He said that because liberty is to faction as air is to fire (because of the real nature of man), therefore republican government, in order to *last*, requires *extensive* territory and population, so that the sheer *multiplicity* of factions might make possible an endless checking and balancing in which an overbearing tyrannical combination would be unlikely.

All of these door-shuttings, all of this limiting, dividing, balancing, and restraining of power, may indeed be said to rest upon a wary and realistic view of human propensities: No person is to be trusted with unrestrained power. Every person should submit his or her will, and each group should submit its will to the criticism and restraint and balance of others— other wills, other interests, other conceptions of the common good. That is half the story of republican government.

It is made clear not only by the instrument itself but also by its authoritative interpretation in the extraordinary series of pieces that its most brilliant defenders produced for a New York newspaper, brought together as *The Federalist*. The best-known quotations from the best-known numbers of *The Federalist* feature the theme of the restraining of power because of the real inclinations of human nature: in *Federalist* 10, the inevitability of divisions into contending groups among human beings in whom self-love distorts reason; in *Federalist* 51, the defense of the separating and interweaving of the branches of the federal government in order that "ambition" may check "ambition." The exclamation that is perhaps the most often quoted of all, from *Federalist* 51, begins by asking, rhetorically: "What is government but the great reflection on human nature?" And, it goes on to say, to paraphrase, that if men were angels they wouldn't need government, but since they aren't, they do. (So Madison says; others would say that even angels need government.) Enlightened statesmen will not always be at the helm, said Madison—therefore don't count on it. Better motives will not always prevail, wrote Madison. Therefore design a system that builds in institutional restraints and protections and that *uses*, instead of *assumes* away, the many varieties of, the consistent presence of, human selfishness.

As we noted above, and as Bryce's quotation implies, this "realism" about humankind is often traced to the religious background of the American colonials—as English Puritans, as Protestants, as products of the many varieties of Reformed Theology.

To be sure, that mighty tradition is certainly not the only one to recognize the dark side of human nature. In an interesting little aside in a debate in Alton, Illinois, during the contest for the Senate seat in that state in 1858, the Republican candidate had occasion to remark: "The Bible says somewhere that we are desperately selfish." But then Lincoln, the witty fellow, drily added: "I think we would have discovered that fact without the Bible." Yes, we would have discovered it, many people *have* discovered it, without the Bible. Thucydides did. Niccoló Machiavelli did. Thomas Hobbes did. The Whigs in England had certainly discovered human selfishness, or at least the danger of all power, to some extent without help from the Bible—and they were one source of the American constitutional thinking. Social philosophers of all times and places, realists everywhere, have known something about it. Human beings of all races and climes have known something about it. As Lincoln implied, that point isn't hard to come by. But the English Puritan preachers and the Dutch Reformed theologians and the others who influenced the American colonials had a more pointed and complex conception, and in a different context—a religious context—that distinguished their view from these others.

The late Sydney Ahlstrom even went so far as to see the American Revolution as the postponed fulfillment, at last, across the Atlantic, of the aborted Puritan Revolution in England. And the English Puritans of New England and elsewhere were not the only source in America of the Reformed tradition, with its rather more insistent doctrine of human sinfulness. When one combines those with a Puritan heritage with the Scotch Irish, the Dutch Reformed, the German Reformed, and the evangelical party in the Church of England, among others, one may find more than 80 percent of the colonists connected to the Reformed tradition.

There are, to be sure, many ways in which we could wish the principle of institutionalized wariness about power, of balancing and checking, could have been continued and applied more thoughtfully to the enormous changes that came with technological development, economic and geographical expansion, and international power. Madison's principle that "where power is, there is the threat to Liberty" applies, obviously, to the powers that have developed since the Constitution was written. The balanced, reflective, carefully reasoned institution-building of the founders, drawing upon a storehouse of Puritan-

Protestant wisdom and other older (and some new) stock as well, was not continued into the life of the new nation. Essentially all of the fundamental and deliberate institution-building went on in this flurry of activity in the late eighteenth century.

For all that—the many other reservations one might have about the particular working of the whole polity under the 200-year-old instrument—the main point still is its success. This complex internal checking and balancing surely has been one reason for the success and longevity of our constitutional system.

What, finally, brought the egregious Senator Joseph McCarthy under control? The instruments of government seemed cowed. But first a new form of communication, television, in the Army-McCarthy hearings revealed the Senator's characteristics in a way that could not be argued with; then the most fundamental of all constitutional controls, an election in 1954, turned control of the Senate from Republicans to Democrats and pitched McCarthy out of his chairmanship; and, third, the Senate, itself as a body offended by this obstreperous member, set up the sober Watkins Committee which then censured him. It took a long time, and it was not the republic's finest hour, but in the end the constitutional system did work.

In the Watergate story one could almost apply the *Federalist* papers item by item: the ambitions of a constitutionally protected free press; the separated power of the Ervin Committee in the Senate; the jealous independence of a Supreme Court, even with a majority appointed by the President's party and a chief appointed by the President himself; the solemn duty of the House Judiciary Committee. Each of these played its role in a peaceful deposing of a Chief Executive, and a transition in power, almost inconceivable in other polities, took place.

To some extent the controversy over the Vietnam War showed the same eventual resilience, and certainly the lasting power, of our complex constitutional system: even a very powerful and adroit and not overly scrupulous Chief Executive in wartime, with all the powers of the modern presidency, had to face such independent bases of power—beyond his rather extensive reach—in the Senate and in the press and in the system of elections, which in the end brought down his party and himself. Whatever its outcome, we may already say that the display of extra-constitutional activity within the executive branch, within the very White House basement, that we are examining as this is written—the so-called Iran-Contra scandals—has already shown some of the same protection in our constitutional system.

But if we reflect, even just on these episodes of recent history, letting alone the entire picture of an experience under the Constitution, we will perceive that there is something more there, in addition to and accompanying the checks and balances. Perhaps the religious tradition had a role in that "something more" as well.

Two: The Constitution Opens the Door

The "checks and balances" are not the sole reason for this Constitution's longevity and success. Surely we cannot explain the nation's constitutional origins,

or its persistence and success, by reference to realism
or the restraint of power alone; those points taken
alone would lead—often do lead—in a quite different
direction from that of the American republican government: to the *Leviathan*, realpolitik, a gridlock of
power groups, cynicism. You cannot explain the
persistence and success, or the nature, of American
government by reference solely to the restraining and
balancing of power; there was in the founding instance the prior fact of a grant of power, along with its
restraint, and without which it would be meaningless—the grant of a particular kind of power.

Prior to our separating, there is the fact of our uniting. Before we can participate in agencies of government that are counterposed, so that each may shut the
door on the other, there must be the single whole and
united government of which they are all a part, opening the door to common purpose. Before ambition is
set against ambition, there must be the common
arena within which these ambitions are juxtaposed
and the implicit common purpose that transcends the
explicit contending purposes. Otherwise the contending powers and interests, contending ambitions,
would rip the polity to pieces, as it has certainly done
elsewhere. It was, of course, exactly the purpose of
the constitution-makers so to design the apparatus of
government as to make these juxtaposed ambitions,
interests, and factions, arising both from the difference among human beings and from their self-love,
serve not chaos or tyranny but liberty and the public
good—and to make them do so in part by the *design* of
their relationship.

The Constitution would not have made it past the first crisis, over the Jay Treaty and the American response to the French Revolution in the 1790s, if balancing were all. In imitation of the American Constitution, constitutions have been written for nations around the world replete with all the restraints on power, all the checks and balances, anybody could ask for, and they have failed. Prior to, and giving meaning to, those *restraints* on power was the *grant* of power—the power to act on behalf of common purposes of an already existing community. Without that commonality and purposiveness the restraining would have been empty or destructive. That balancing takes place within a prior and supervening mutual engagement—an engagement to each other to make one people and to serve the shared good and to seek and define it by mutual persuasion.

This shared and reciprocal engagement has its connection, too, to the republicanized Christianity and Christianized republicanism that shaped this nation's mind.

One important representation of that connection goes all the way back to those original Americans making their errand into the wilderness by means of the *Arbella* and her sister ships, listening there to their Governor hold forth about how they were going to have all the eyes of the world upon them. Winthrop's speech on *The Model of Christian Charity* features an understanding of the whole people "knit together in the bond of brotherly affection" that stands rather sharply in contrast to the outlook of some of those who would later sentimentally appropriate his phrase about a city on a hill. "We must be willing to abridge ourselves of our superfluities for the supply of others' necessities," said Winthrop.

> "We must delight in each other, make others' conditions our own, rejoice together, mourn together, labor and suffer together, always having before our eyes our Commission and Community in the work, our Community as members of the same body, so shall we keep the unity of the spirit in the bond of peace . . ."

Winthrop's speech reverberates with phrases and figures emphasizing the commonality, the community, the shared and reciprocal obligation, the fundamental and original moral interweaving of life with life and the obligation that follows therefrom.

Although there were other and different traditions woven into the spiritual tapestry of the new nation, in addition to New England Puritanism, they were all more or less communitarian. Both republicanism and the Christian religion, under which headings we can group most of the formative influences on the original United States, were communitarian.

The United States has in fact rested upon more of a communal core than its more recent ideologies have acknowledged, and upon a deeper and more complex understanding of our relationships to each other and of each of us to the polity, than a simple reference to checks and balances, of power balancing power, would imply or our more recent individualism comprehend.

Just at the time of the Revolution and the Constitution-making, this communitarianism was extending out from the states to embrace the larger emerging nation. Behind the Constitution is the Declaration of Independence, that moment when the United States was besouled, at the end of which there was pledged, in a perfect phrase, our lives, our fortunes, and our sacred honor, and at the beginning of which, before the theory of government and before the list of grievances against the King, there is in the first line the assumption that makes the whole case already, that we are one people. And then in the second paragraph of the besouling document, there is a restatement of the universal purpose of which this one people is a bearer and representative—a universal purpose which four score and seven years later the greatest of Americans, who said he drew his whole political philosophy from the Declaration of Independence, restated with incomparable power.

Behind the Declaration of Independence, there was a century and a half of experience of the people working out the meaning of the compacts and covenants and pledges they had made on their original errands into wilderness. Surrounding the Revolutionary events, more important in the end than the grievances, gripes, and protests about stamps, tea, declaratory acts, and the behavior of Royal governors, was the revolution that would take place—had already taken place, by the time of the Revolution—in the minds of the people that had made them one.

The Constitution provided the instruments of national government in a way that the Articles of Confederation had not done, and that leading shapers and defenders of the new federal Constitution had as a first priority.

These founders wanted a government, first of all, that could govern. After the experience of the Articles of Confederation—trying to cajole the states into anteing up the money for the Continental Army—they wanted a central government, a national government that was strong, that could govern. Certainly that was true of Alexander Hamilton, the most important figure in the movement to call the Philadelphia convention, and also of James Madison, the most important single figure perhaps in that Convention, and of James Wilson, its unsung hero, and of Gouverneur Morris, its stylist, and of the silent presiding officer, George Washington, and of the dominant group, the "nationalists." They had learned, and not only from books, what evils weak governments led to. The new government must *first* be able to govern the people—to shut the door, so to speak, on all of us.

But also, then, the government must be able to govern itself. The checks and balances may be seen as the devices by means of which it does that. (A government that can govern—and be governed, is a paraphrase of yet another well-known sentence from Madison's entries in the *Federalist* series.)

One certainly can find, in the times of our national beginnings, antecedents and anticipations of that hostility to goverment as such, to all government, to the very principle of government, that was to become an important theme in the American political culture of the nineteenth and twentieth centuries and virtually its only theme in the 1980s. In the great pamphlet *Common Sense*, in which Tom Paine caught the moment when the American colonials were ready to be persuaded to go on from protest for rights as Englishmen to a revolution for independence as Americans and helped to persuade them to make that step, Tom Paine distinguished "society" from "government" in a way that is unfavorable to the latter. The great speeches of Patrick Henry, another and earlier rousing of popular feeling against the mother country's "oppression," included much antigovernmental material, and Henry would revert to those themes when he led the fight against ratifying the Philadelphia Constitution. Thomas Jefferson, of course, is often pictured as having been systematically antigovernmental, although a more complete and sophisticated understanding of his thought might qualify that popular view. No doubt the slogan attributed to him, about the least government being the best government, does indeed have roots and persistence in American political thinking. It does have a religious home, as it were, in the come-outer and sectarian spirit, withdrawing from and attacking all institutions of this world, government above all, and in the individualism and voluntaryism, in implicit political philosophy as well as in explicit piety and theology and church polity and morals, which marked the spread of the free and revivalistic churches in the first half of the nineteenth century. That pious individualism of religious origin would then become entangled with the economic individualism of political economy and burgeoning capitalism in the last half of the nineteenth century to form an ideological complex with the consequences of which we are still living.

But at the time of the founding, those developments were still to come. Whatever there was of all antigovernmental impulse and of individualism was set in the different context of opposition to British rule, to empire, to the remnants of feudalism. And—they lost. If they had not, we would not be here. May we not interpret the writing and ratifying of the United States Constitution as the victory of those who affirmed energetic republican government over those hostile to all government?

In Forrest McDonald's book on the intellectual origins of the Constitution, *Novus Ordo Seclorum*, he starts by identifying "a crucial step toward becoming able to devise a viable system of free political institutions," namely, "the perception that energetic government is necessary to the security of liberty and property." He quotes James Madison: "'the more lax the bond,' the more easily can the strong devour the weak." That is one part, the negative part, of the republican justification of energetic government: because "where power is, there is the threat to liberty," as Madison said elsewhere, and even in those simpler days of a largely agricultural economy not all "power" that threatens liberty was concentrated in governmental institutions. McDonald—describing the situation of the Americans of 1787, as the delegates assembled for the Philadelphia convention—goes on to say: "Patriots had tended to view the problem as having only one dimension, that of preventing oppression by government. Now they could see a second dimension." McDonald then proceeds to cite a quotation from Benjamin Rush that makes use, in his own way, of that metaphor about opening and shutting doors that we took from Bryce and used above. Rush— quoted by McDonald—said: "In our opposition to monarchy, we forget that the temple of tyranny has two doors. We bolted one of them by proper restraints; but we left the other open, by neglecting the guard against the effects of our own ignorance and licentiousness." In other words—to interpret this now in our own running metaphor—though throughout government there must be all these door-shuttings, there must also be energetic government to carry on the further door-shuttings against all of us, all other centers of power, against the strong devouring the weak, against our own taking advantage of each other.

An Alexander Hamilton at least would then go further: Energetic government was essential to republican government not only to prevent the evils arising from other centers of power but also to accomplish the positive common purposes that made republicanism real—to open doors to common purposes.

The government, though "energetic," must itself be governed by the people even as it governs them, the whole making through its intricacies a circle that may be described as self-government—in the phrase of the greatest of Americans government of, by, and for the people. It is as much to break that circle to deny the principle of government—to undercut and demean it, and treat it cynically—as to break out of the restraints in extralegal adventures and tyrannies.

The whole of the constitutional system is imbued with respect for fundamental law, for law beyond the particular laws, for what the document itself calls "The Supreme Law of the Land." We Americans at our founding invented this quite new conception, that the whole people in an original and independent action prior and superior to particular legislation established a permanent superior written instrument, a Supreme Law, a Constitution governing the government. This is an embodiment of the original and permanent constituting action of the whole people, which action is superior to all particular acts of particular agents of government, empowering and defining but also restraining them. Thus, to the bafflement at least of many from other countries, and sometimes of our own citizens as well, it is altogether possible that in the name of this permanent and superior action of the whole people some particular action of "the people" (of today's legislature, today's majority) can be struck down—declared unconstitutional.

Which among our original institutions most clearly embodies the essence of republican government? Congress does. One republican advantage of a legislative body is that each of these egos must meet other egos who are also Senators, also Representatives, also state legislators, also aldermen. All of these are interested parties and power-seekers, and all of these are (the same people) also bearers of different goods, values, and visions. There is a kind of "checking and balancing" in that, if you will, a restraint of the ego of each by the ego of the other and of the collected others. But that is only the underside: there is also, in theory, and sometimes also in practice, an exchange of ideas, arguments, and conceptions of what is good, a conversation, a deliberation, out of which comes a corporate decision—that process described by the prophet Isaiah and President Lyndon B. Johnson as "come, let us reason together." That mutual persuasion (and mutual restraining) in making law is at the heart of the nature of a republic, of a democracy.

Congress and other legislatures, even the New Haven Board of Aldermen, are central symbols of republican life in a way that Presidents, Governors, armies, bureaucrats, sheriffs, and even (abstracted from the nature of the legal system) judges are not; antirepublican regimes have all of these. But such regimes do not have genuine legislatures filtering the larger reasoning of a public composing the laws.

Take also a jury, an old and central institution of a free society. The accused peers—not superiors—chosen without favoritism, in enough numbers hear the evidence and arguments and then withdraw to a room and pick their first among equals and then reason together until they reach a decision. The American public does have an understanding, not too cynical, of juries.

And it has the habits of majority rule. In another less republicanized culture, a defeated candidate, having said and heard all those extreme things, heads for the hills and takes out the guns. Our majoritarianism is too little qualified by respect for the civil freedom under which alone a majority has moral dignity (that is, the ever-present possibility that any temporary majority can be talked and voted out of its status) and is too much conceived as sheer numbers. (Don't talk—VOTE.) But it is nevertheless real and one aspect of republican government.

Our arguments are a sign that we agree—our rationally articulated disagreements at one level are a sign that we have agreements at a higher level. We have shared reference points with respect to which we can argue and shared ground rules and means with which we can argue and a shared community—a larger commitment to each other—within which we can argue. Those who take themselves outside that community, who reject those higher common reference points and those shared means and ground rules, who grab a gun literally or figuratively, or who flee or withdraw or undercut the common agreements, John Courtney Murray called "barbarians," in a strict use of the word, and said they were barbarians still even if they wore Brooks Brothers suits while composing advertising copy with an expensive pencil. We are at our best, as he said, a community "locked in argument."

Three: The Failure and Success of the Constitution

Lord Bryce, in the passage already cited, went on to make a contrast between the hearty Puritanism of the American Constitution and the optimism and enthusiasm of the comparable French instruments during and after the French Revolution: Power used and restrained was not a central point for them.

The French experience is a good "control", as the social scientists say, a comparison to test what is distinctive, for our American "revolution." (If you are an alderman in New Haven, your "control" is Bridge-port.)

Let us look at a speech that captures something about that other revolution, perhaps at its worst, in order to dramatize the contrast that Bryce was making. This is the speech that Robespierre gave to the French convention of February 5, 1794, after the Revolution had turned on itself, turned bloody.

> "But to found and consolidate democracy, we must first end the war of liberty against tyranny, and traverse the storm of the Revolution. . . .
>
> "We must crush both the interior and exterior enemies of the republic, or perish with her. And in this situation, the first maxim of your policy should be to conduct the people by reason and the enemies of the people by terror.
>
> "If the spring of popular government during peace is virtue, the spring of popular government during rebellion is virtue, and terror; virtue, without which terror is fatal! Terror, without which virtue is powerless! Terror is nothing else than justice, prompt, secure, and inflexible!
>
> "It is, therefore, an emanation of virtue; it is less a particular principle than a consequence of the general principles of democracy, applied to the most urgent wants of the country."

He is saying that since you by definition represent "democracy" and Liberty, Equality, Fraternity—in fact everything, including all virtues and the

Good—you may (or must!) use *Terror* to consolidate that virtue!

Robespierre, perhaps a little uneasily, hears some reservations about that and responds:

> "It has been said that terror is the instrument of a despotic government. Does yours then resemble despotism? Yes, as the sword which glitters in the hand of a hero of liberty resembles that with which the satellites of tyranny are armed!
>
> "The government of a revolution is the despotism of liberty against tyranny. Is force, then, only made to protect crime? It is not also made to strike haughty heads which the lightning has doomed? . . .
>
> ". . . it is necessary that one or the other should succumb. Indulgence for the Royalist! exclaimed certain people. Pardon for wretches! No! Pardon for innocence, pardon for the weak, pardon for the unhappy, pardon for humanity!"

Is it unfair to suggest that something like the attitude expressed in this speech marks others of the world revolutions, to some extent in the nineteenth century, but then overwhelmingly in the twentieth?

Characteristically, such revolutionary ideology posits a New Humanity *after* the revolution, when the limitations of present humanity will be overcome. It justifies today's cruelty in the name of that radical newness, that new social order, even that new kind of human being, that will arise *after* the revolution. The Puritanized Republicanism of the United States had in it still enough of the two-worldliness of the Christian heritage, soaked into the ethos and built into the institutions, to avoid the worst forms of that cruel utopianism: Any social order so radically new as to transfer humankind, a new Jerusalem, a New Heaven and a New Earth, will not be entirely of this world, nor the result of merely human activities.

The more radical revolutionary temper also categorically and absolutely separates itself from an opposition, the enemies of the revolution, the enemies of the people ("enemies of the republic . . . Royalists . . . wretches") against whom the most extreme measures are justified, by the presumed radical newness the revolution will achieve. The Anglo-American temper, by contrast, did not allow itself so sharp a division of humankind.

Of course, there are historical and social conditions that made the American "revolution," the breaking away from England to set up a new independent nation, much "easier" than the French and Russian Revolutions, or the Iranian and many others, for that matter. Nevertheless, ideas and beliefs *do* matter enormously. The ideas and beliefs surrounding the American founding gave us an ideological climate different from that reflected in Robespierre's speech. And we can say that a chief source of that difference was the Puritan heritage of suspicion of all human power, which included an introspective criticism of one's own power. When Puritanism lacked or would lose the elements of unversality and self-criticism, it would turn into an engine of inhumanity, too, but it had the possibility in it of a checking and balancing going even deeper than any constitutional system, which could then make institutions reflecting such restraints continue to live.

A pattern for reciprocal restraints, an instrument of shared commitment, a design for mutual persuasion—the American constitutional system, considered in its larger moral and symbolic meaning, is all of these. But it is, or has become, something more: the charter for a continuing, an expanding, fulfillment of humane possibilities.

This point may be illustrated by reference to the most serious immediate failure of the American Constitution-makers. Two hundred years ago Jemmy Madison was sitting there in Montpelier looking at the constitutions of ancient and modern republics. He and his generation were, in Edmund Randolph's phrase, "children of the revolution." They had come to adulthood in a moment of high human excitement and adventure, a revolution, in which they had repeatedly used, as a primary moral claim, the word "Liberty," and very often, too, as its negation and opposite, the words "slaves" and "slavery": "The British with their tax on tea, their stamp act, cannot make of us *slaves*." Madison himself, writing there in Montpelier two and a half years before the Philadelphia convention, in the early summer of 1784 had written in his great *Memorial and Remonstrance*: "People who submit to . . . laws made neither by themselves nor by an authority derived from them, are slaves." That was the language, the imagery, of the patriots: "Liberty" was their cause, these sons of Liberty; "Slavery" was the condition to which submission to the British Parliament, and finally to the British King, would reduce them.

Somewhere else in the house, and out in the tobacco fields and in the barn, there were people with black faces, preparing the meals, curing the tobacco, caring for the horses, bringing Madison his meals while he wrote his words on behalf of Liberty, getting his horse ready for him to ride to meetings where the patriots would condemn the "slavery" to which the British proposed to reduce them. And so it was also with Thomas Jefferson, thirty miles to the South at Monticello, where the slave quarters are decorously hidden in the architecture, and up North at Gunston Hall, with Virginia's "Mr. Human Rights," George Mason, and over on the hill overlooking a great bend in the Potomac, with the father of his country, at Mount Vernon.

How did it sound to the ears of the black persons who served the tables while the Sons of Liberty grew furious with the British at the "slavery" to which they would reduce their fellows by a requirement of a stamp on paper or of a 3 pence tax on tea?

The first census, in 1790, counted 3.9 million Americans; of these 697,000 were bound in a perpetual and hereditary form of chattel slavery founded upon racial distinction—about as sharp a contradiction to the ideals of the revolution as could be imagined. Many of the best known of the founders were troubled by the contradiction between their revolutionary libertarian and egalitarian claims and the institution of human slavery in their own midst. Among them were James Madison, who at one point in his life hoped to arrange his finances so that he would not be dependent upon slavery for his own economic base, but who, preoccupied with his single-minded life-long service to building a new country, was never able to do it; Thomas Jefferson, whose paragraph about slavery—"I tremble when I remember God is Just"—was often to be quoted; and George Washington, who actually did better than the other two when it came to manumitting his own slaves in his will. Madison, we learn from Adrienne Koch, very much respected—perhaps there was a wistful moral envy—a relative of Dolley's who repudiated the whole slave-based life, moved out of the slave-holding states, and opposed the institution. George Mason, owner of 200 slaves, was an abolitionist.

In Philadelphia, the founders made tortured compromises with slavery in the Constitution. There was the ridiculous 3/5ths clause, the so-called federal ratio—without which, Madison later said, it would not have been possible to get the Constitution ratified. There was also the provision in Article IV, section 2, that gave apparent constitutional sanction to the concept of a fugitive slave. Finally, as part of the other side of the compromise, there was the provision in Article I, section 9, setting the date for the ending of slave trade.

The story of this aspect of the work of our Founding Fathers is not told as often as perhaps it ought to be. During the bicentennial of the Constitution, it fell to the one black Justice on the Supreme Court, in the midst of much rather empty celebrating, to raise this central question. How did these heroes of our national founding, building a new society based on human liberty, cope, or not cope, with the fact of human slavery in their midst?

The story is well told in *Slavery in the Structure of American Politics*, by Donald Robinson of Smith College. Did our forefathers distinguish themselves on this question? No. Does the story do them credit? No. After telling the story of the debates on the slave trade, with Pinckney and Butler of South Carolina, on their side, adamant and energetic, and the others, who were neither, Robinson refers to the "unequal tension that produced the Constitution's provisions on slavery: the clarity and determination of those with a direct interest versus the relative ignorance and unconcern of those without this direct interest."

Here is a summary paragraph from Robinson, indicating one scholar's conception of what might have been done, or tried. He writes,

"On the question of the representation of states in Congress, many Northerners had shown themselves willing to take the Convention to the edge of collapse. One cannot help wondering what concessions could have been wrung from the slaveholders if a similar will had been shown to limit the power of slavery. Could slavery have been confined to 'states now existing'? Could the rights of free Negroes have been defined and secured? Could the rights of owners who wished to emancipate their chattels have been established against state laws to the contrary? It is impossible to say, because the Convention never really broached these subjects. The most perceptive delegates acknowledged the power of slavery to cleave the

union in two, but the Convention as a whole failed
to regard this fact as a challenge to their moral and
political imagination."

Robinson goes on to generalize about the attitude
of our Founding Fathers—our constitution-writers—
about slavery.

"Most of the framers were either unperturbed
about slavery or else completely resigned to its
presence in America. None saw slavery as a
sufficient moral or political evil to justify even a
careful analysis of its effects, much less a stand
against its continued existence. These men—who
had shown themselves capable of the most imagi-
native political thinking and the boldest political
action on other issues—were willing to acquiesce
in slavery for two reasons: because the suffering of
Negroes did not sufficiently quicken their sym-
pathies, and because they were unable to imagine
a viable alternative."

Perhaps the role of James Madison on this issue,
taken as a whole, cannot be much separated from the
failure of the group. But he was a leader at least in this
regard: He was first among those who insisted at
every point that the *word* "slavery" and its cognates
not appear in the Constitution—that the Constitution
not recognize that there could be "property in men."
And the avoidance of the words "slavery" and "slave"
in the Constitution was not a small matter; it did have
consequences. It did mean that later there could be
the argument, most importantly by Abraham Lincoln,

that the founders, by this careful omission as well as in other ways, intended *not* to recognize slavery, but merely to acquiesce in its necessity and to put it on the road to ultimate extinction.

A half century later, the moral energy and imagination the founders lacked was found elsewhere—in the revived Christianity of the period of the Second Awakening.

The opposition to slavery had always centered in the churches, from the first antislavery protest by German pietists in Germantown, Pennsylvania, in 1688. Quakers furnished the most widespread anti-slavery leadership in the middle of the eighteenth century; the Philadelphia meeting in 1758 urged all Quakers to free their slaves, and in 1775 the first antislavery organization was founded in Philadelphia. (Benjamin Franklin was a member.) Two ministers in the Edwards' strain of the Reformed tradition preached against slavery in the 1770s: Samuel Hopkins in Newport and Jonathan Edwards, Jr., in New Haven.

In the records of the Philadelphia convention of 1787, there are interesting backhanded reflections of the role of the churches, and of religious conviction, in opposition to slavery—backhanded because they appear in remarks by the *supporters* of slavery. They knew that there was an association between religion and their opponents. Rutledge of South Carolina said (according to Madison's notes) that

"religion and humanity had nothing to do with this question. Interest alone is the governing principle with nations. The true question at present is whether the Southern states shall or shall not be parties to the Union."

In the process of ratification, General Pinckney of South Carolina, who had been a delegate, speaking on behalf of ratification of the Constitution in Charleston, explained to his fellow South Carolinians that when he and his Southern colleagues had dealt with the slave trade question in the Philadelphia convention, they had had to contend with "the religious and political prejudices" of New England and Pennsylvania. Finally, as a result of their deliberations, Pinckney said, the Northern delegates promised "to restrain the religious and political prejudices" of their constituents on the issue.

There were objections to the Constitution, among opponents of slavery, in the process of ratification. But it was ratified and began its course through modern history.

The "religious prejudices" against slavery grew, and in the second quarter of the nineteenth century they swept across the nation. At first, in the 1820s and 1830s, the most active abolition societies were in the South, but then the mind of the region closed defensively around its peculiar institution. The source of the assault, South and North, was the churches, the Christian population, particularly the outpouring from the new wave of revivals. Out of the Finney revivals and Lane Seminary and New England's reform impulse, from Theodore Weld's preaching and the organizing and agitating of hundreds of preachers and laymen, there came the most consequential of all the reform movements of the nineteenth-century

America. The daughter, wife, and sister of clergymen, with a tract by an evangelist under her pillow, wrote as if inspired the "good bad book," as George Orwell called it, that was surely the most influential social tract ever written in America—*Uncle Tom's Cabin.* The varieties of abolition and antislavery in nineteenth-century American Protestantism were not always wise or imbued with discriminate judgment; they indulged in some moral exhibitionism, and they did at times exhibit the bane of self-righteousness; with the amendments ending slavery after the Civil War, many of them did feel simplistically that the problem was solved. Reading the materials of that time, one can feel some of the leaders of "social Christianity" (to use that term) checking that issue off and going on to the next. In other words, one doubts that the leaders of these movements could have framed a wise and balanced instrument of government that would last, and serve republican values, for 200 years. Nevertheless, they had something else. Robinson writes that the

> "ideology of natural rights [by which he means the dominant philosophy or philosophies of the founders] was a formidable weapon in the hands of people who were hurting and who sought to explain their hurt. But it seemed to have little capacity to propel the imagination, to induce men to care about or feel the slavery of others . . . slavery faced a more serious challenge in the 19th century, when a public philosophy that gave a larger place to human compassion began to have its sway."

The "public philosophy" Robinson is referring to is the social reform impulse evaluating from the churches.

But, in a sense, the constitutional system designed by the first group was able to accommodate the radical change in the society—the abolition of slavery—promoted by the second group. It was and it was not. On the one had, it was necessary to pass through the "terrible scourge" of a bloody Civil War, the first modern war, to resolve the differences over slavery and Union. On the other hand, the constitutional system, much altered (and improved—brought into accord with the underlying ideals) by the Thirteenth, Fourteenth, and Fifteenth Amendments and all that surrounds them, did survive and grow and continue to our own time.

One hundred years, more or less, after the Civil War, the United States, under its original Constitution, was able to turn the law around with respect to racial segregation. To be sure, the "lost hundred years," as C. Vann Woodward has called it, is a large blot on the nation's history, and the United States Constitution did not protect the nation, or the newly freed black citizens, from it. On the contrary: Court interpretations of the Constitution, particularly in 1896, gave the prestige and imprimatur of the Constitution to the iniquitous system of racial segregation by law. A constitution—*any* constitution, any words on paper, (mere "parchment barriers," as James Madison called them), any formal arrangement of institutions—is not self-executing. The Constitution is always, of course, at the mercy of the moral qualities of the people who use it. It is not, it cannot be, no constitution can be, "a machine that would go of itself." But that is not to say the words on paper, the formal arrangements of institutions, are unimportant. If drawn from the consonant with the ideals and the experience of a people, such words and formal arrangements can protect and reinforce the people's better side and encourage its further development. The United States Constitution (as understood by human beings, by judges) has not prevented, and has sometimes vindicated and protected, the evils of American history: to the natives of this continent; to women; to the "strangers in the land"—Catholic and Jewish immigrants from Europe, Chinese in San Francisco and the railroad town of the West, and (perhaps most shocking and clear-cut) the Japanese-Americans in World War II. The Constitution (as judges of a certain stripe interpreted it) did not prevent the economic miseries and injustices that arose as the nation moved from its original rural agricultural base to become an urban industrial giant; to the contrary, it was used to strike down efforts by social idealism to correct these evils. The Constitution has been only a partial and intermittent barrier to the evils that have arisen in its most sacred inner temple—freedom of thought, of opinion, of political argument, as in the periods of national hysteria and repression after World Wars I and II. All of which is to say—to repeat—that this Constitution cannot—no constitution can—operate untouched by human hands. Every such constitutional instrument, as every human institution, is simply the form and the beginning, to which human beings as free moral agents give substance and continuation.

But if the Constitution offered, and could offer, no magical solutions to the moral dilemmas of the people that would live under it, leaving them free of course to form themselves, often badly, and to shape their attitudes, often reprehensible ones, and to develop lesser institutions, often contrary to the Constitution's spirit, and to make the decisions of life, often wrongly, it was nevertheless there to be used for, and to re-inforce, the "better angels of our nature," when these should show themselves again. The story of the Civil Rights Movement of 1954-1968, or 1948-1968, or 1941-1965—the modern Civil Rights Movement—is by no means a story of the Constitution only, but it is nevertheless in a very important and indispensible part a story of the constitution. For many decades, the NAACP and others fought through the courts to alter the law—to restore the Constitution's integrity—and on May 19, 1954, after earlier preliminary victories, the Supreme Court unanimously found racially segre-gated schools to be inherently unequal. In other words, it found in the Constitution the nation's premise of equality, correcting the popular century-long, centuries-long, denial. That decision, and all that surrounds it, is of course the greatest vindication of the constitutional system in our times, though not the only one.

One does not want to be complacent, and the criterion here implicitly employed is a minimal one—did the system survive with its core values in-tact? But by the real standards of human life on this planet, the extravagant positive things said about the American Constitution have some truth in them. Two hundred years of modern history is a long time. The

United States has been able to unfold from the original thirteen states all the way across the continent out to the Pacific to make forty-eight states, and then out into the ocean and up into the frozen north to gather in two more, from a nation of four million on the Atlantic coast to a nation of 250 million stretching to, and out into, the Pacific. It has grown from a cluster of colonies on the margin of Europe to a dominant world power. In this century, the United States has been able to move from the periphery of the European power system to the unquestioned center of the world stage, to operate here as the first nation with weapons capable of world destruction, in the midst of ideological fury of the twentieth century, with the constitutional system so far still intact. The United States and its subordinate units have made their way under this Constitution through an unbroken string of regularly scheduled elections from George Washington to the present incumbent, from the First Congress to the One Hundredth. We managed to hold genuine elections in the middle of a Civil War in 1864, in the depths of a depression in 1932, after the assassination in 1964 and the resignation in 1976, as well as during both world wars. In this difficult time, since World War II, in which the once small and isolated nation has now come to be a gigantic power with its fingers reaching around the globe, we have weathered several episodes that had overtones of threat to the polity, in which it can be said, I believe, that something like the original system of mutual persuasion, shared commitment, and reciprocal restraints—extended—actually did work. This system has continued through Civil War, Depression, World War, assassinations, and a Presidential resignation, which is no small triumph, as human history goes. If it can carry the principles it represents onto the world stage in the years to come, then we will really prove to have been a New Order for the Ages.

COMPLEXITY'S CHALLENGE TO FEDERALISM: A BICENTENNIAL LOOK TO THE FUTURE

by

Patrick E. Higginbotham

Patrick E. Higginbotham

Patrick E. Higginbotham was born on December 16, 1938, in McCalla, Alabama, and attended public schools in Alabama. He attended the University of Texas at Arlington and at Austin and received his B.A. and LL.B. degrees from the University of Alabama. He served as note editor of the Law Review, an officer of the student body, a member of the national moot court team and was elected to membership in the Bench and Bar Legal Honor Society and Omicron Delta Kappa. Following graduation from law school he served for three years as a member of the JAG-Airforce.

He then practiced with the Dallas law firm of Coke & Coke, where his work was confined to trials and appeals, with one stint as a special prosecutor. In 1975, he was appointed to the United States District Court, Northern District of Texas, by President Ford. He was then the youngest sitting federal judge in the United States. In 1982, he was appointed to the United States Court of Appeals, Fifth Circuit, by President Reagan and now serves on that court.

Judge Higginbotham served for four years as a faculty member of the Federal Judicial Center. He is an Adjunct Professor of Law at Southern Methodist University Law School, where he has taught courses in federal practice and now teaches constitutional law; at SMU, he has served as a member of the Board of Visitors, as chairman of the search committee for endowed chairs, and as advisor to the Southwestern Law Journal.

He is a member of the Farrah Law Society, the Order of the Coif, the American Law Institute, and a Fellow of the American Bar Foundation, a Director of the Dallas Bar Foundation, a judicial member of the council of the Antitrust Section of the American Bar Association, a director of the American Judicature Society and is a Research Fellow and Trustee of the Southwestern Legal Foundation.

COMPLEXITY'S CHALLENGE TO FEDERALISM:
A BICENTENNIAL LOOK TO THE FUTURE

by

Patrick E. Higginbotham

In 1985, the Chief Judge of the United States Court of Appeals for the Fifth Circuit, joined by four judges, suggested the creation of a federal common law for asbestos cases within the Fifth Circuit, persuaded that the interstate nature of the controversy made the application of state law "inappropriate," As I will explain, asbestos cases are one of a genre of cases grown from a common seed, the complexity of which sorely taxes our court system. The extraordinary nature of the proposal to create a federal common law for asbestosis cases emphasizes the difficulties they pose.

In *Jackson v. Johns-Manville Sales Corp.*, we detailed the dimensions of the asbestos problem. (750 F.2d 1314, 1336 [5th Cir. 1985]. We noted that in August 1982 approximately 21,000 claimants had filed product liability suits alleging asbestos-related injury, and that within seven months the figure had grown to 24,000, with new suits being added at an average rate of 500 per month. We pointed out that in the 1970s this country consumed between 608,000 and 876,000 short tons of asbestos commonly found in the home and work environments, that exposure to even small amounts can result in asbestos-related disease, including mesothelioma, a fatal cancer. To compound the difficulty, the disease frequently is latent from between fifteen to forty years. One Department of Labor study estimated that more than 21 million living American workers had been exposed to asbestos over the preceding four years, and some 200,000 deaths before the year 2000 are anticipated. The Epidemiology Research Institute estimates that Johns-Manville faces between 30,000 and 120,000 suits. The Rand Corporation calculated that defendant asbestos companies paid claimants some $400 million dollars between 1970 and 1982. The cases are proceeding in at least forty-eight states, with slightly more than one-half of all cases pending in federal courts, and in 1982, 39 percent of those were pending in the Fifth Circuit.

Persons suffering injury from exposure to asbestos do not face a uniform system of rules. To the contrary, the laws of the states vary in significant ways in their treatment of such issues as how long a person has in which to file a claim, what he must prove to demonstrate liability, as well as the nature of damages he may recover. Despite strikingly overlapping factual patterns, claims are processed as discrete events, each trial requiring the explanation of medical and scientific problems common to thousands of other cases. Unfortunately, we cannot assume that asbestos litigation is a unique plague. To some measure it is representative of new litigation that transcends political boundaries and forces us to rethink traditional approaches toward the decision of cases. In short, the asbestosis phenomenon may be a paradigm.

My objective is to explain the way in which these

cases—and the resulting call for creation of federal common law—implicate a decisional matrix of concerns related to federalism and the proper role of courts in society. Within this broader framework is a cluster of principles which includes the use of precedent, choice-of-law, full faith and credit, and relatedly, issue and claim preclusion. My task is to explore how these principles can best be accommodated with the fair and efficient disposition of complex cases such as the asbestosis litigation.

At the outset it is helpful to look briefly at some of the components of the matrix and their relationship to each other. One category of concerns focuses on efficiency: the economical administration of complex cases should avoid repetitious trials on common issues of law and fact. This serves both to conserve judicial resources and to give consistency and accuracy to judicial decisions. Several existing mechanisms further this goal. Cases with common parties and issues are consolidated and administered jointly. In the federal system, a statute provides for consolidation where related claims arise in different judicial districts. Even more important, modern rules of issue and claim preclusion give effect to judicial determinations which can extend beyond the parties to a suit. And at the most basic level, the doctrine of stare decisis serves to prevent relitigation of decisions of law.

Other components of our decisional matrix relate to the fact that complex suits often bring into play the interests of several governments. By their nature, complex suits often raise issues that cross state boundaries, thus implicating the competing policies of different states. These suits also bring into play potentially conflicting interests of the states and the federal government. By necessity, our federalist structure is an important factor affecting the adjudication of this new breed of cases.

What I aim to point out is that these two categories of considerations, efficiency in administration and division of authority, contain both internal tensions and tensions between each other. For example, efficient administration must be balanced against the right of each litigant to a day in court. The consolidations of cases and the application of the rules of preclusion at some point may deprive an interested government the opportunity to make its own determination.

What we have, then, is a complicated, dynamic structure whose components might be manipulated to better accommodate complex litigation. The proposal for a federal common law of asbestosis is an example of such manipulation; it would transfer the lawmaking responsibility in such cases to a new unit of government. The question for this paper is the extent to which this proposal, and its alternatives, requires dislocation of the other components of the matrix.

I will first offer a verbal snapshot of the United States in 1787 in order to point out the forces of the change that have been generated by our nation's growth. I will explain how these forces, powerful as they are, have not required any fundamental alteration of the Constitution's assignment of power. I will then describe the debate over the role of federal courts in the maintenance of structure, focusing on stare decisis, selection of state law, and principles of preclusion. Finally, I will return to our model of asbestosis cases, the problems attending their trial, and the difficulties of responding to these problems within this decisional matrix.

I

A Look at 1787

The primary components of our matrix have been in place for some time and emerge from the Constitution's original text. So a good starting point is the question, why should complex litigation only now become a problem for the judiciary? To explain why, it is instructive to look at America in 1787 as the Colliers did in their recent book, *Decision In Philadelphia*. They point out, "the huge size of the country meant that few Americans travel very far very often." A trip of 50 miles was rare at the same time. They point out that in 1790 the population center was 25 miles east of Baltimore, that not more than 10 percent of the population lived in anything that could be called a city or a town. By the time of the Philadelphia Convention, only 5.4 percent of the population lived in places of 2,500 people or more, and 90 percent of white American men were farmers. The population was relatively homogenous, with over 25 percent of the population of British and Irish stock in a country overwhelmingly protestant. America was then seen at home and abroad as a place too large to be governed as a unit.

Not surprisingly, in 1787 the role for the federal government was limited, a role sufficient to overcome

the powerless confederation. As Madison put it in
Federalist 45:

> "The powers delegated by the proposed Constitu-
> tion to the federal government are few and
> defined. Those which are to remain in the State
> governments are numerous and indefinite. The
> former will be exercised principally on external
> objects, as war, peace, negotiation, and foreign
> commerce; with which last the power of taxation
> will, for the most part, be connected. The powers
> reserved to the several States will extend to all the
> objects which, in the ordinary course of affairs,
> concern the lives, liberties, and properties of the
> people, and the internal order, improvement, and
> prosperity of the State."

Lawrence M. Freedman, in his *History of American Law,* explains that the New Deal is probably "the
best and sharpest illustration of the way government
grew in response to consumer demand." He points
out that before Franklin D. Roosevelt, a federal
budget of $80 billion a year was inconceivable—in his
words, "science fiction." The budget of Health and
Human Services alone in the mid-1980s is on the
order of $84 billion. Yet, as Freedman points out, the
decline of state government has been relative and not
absolute; states still "build roads, run schools, operate
the welfare system, hire policemen and firemen, issue
marriage licenses, and grant divorces."

Numerous examples can be summoned to illustrate
the changes over the past 200 years in our life-styles

and the plain demands for central government. The fascination for me is not with the power of the centripetal and nationalizing forces of population growth, increased ethnicity, centralized news, and the like, but rather I am amazed that local government has retained its vitality in the face of this flow. With the welfare system, for example, the dollar flow has been to Washington, but the political forces have clung to local control over the distribution of money. Much of private law—including the areas of contract, tort, zoning, and family relations—is administered by the states. Given the heavy controlling flow through the year of the New Deal, the reality that local government has retained so much suggests that federalism has a core value that transcends the force of centralization.

The Structure Created in 1787

Students in high school civics are familiar with the Constitution's distribution of power among the three branches of government and with its systems of checks and balances. Perhaps they are also aware of the effort by the framers to limit the power of the federal government, find a place for the role of states, and otherwise disperse power by the structural arrangement of a newly seen republic. For me, the true genius of the constitutional arrangement, and the most significant reason for its 200 years of success, is its departure from the structure of republics that had preceded it. This critical departure recognized the corrupting force of power and man's Janus-faced capacity for good and evil. Its antidote was dispersal of power. Simply put, at nigh every turn there is a structure that requires the accommodation of distinct views.

The point I wish to highlight here is the Constitution's heavy dependence upon its structural arrangements as a device for securing liberty. Hobbes explained that freedom is political power divided into small fragments. That teaching finds expression in the two distinct ways of securing liberty in our constitutional arrangement. The more frequently identified aspect of this arrangement today is a system of positively assured protections such as free speech, trial by jury, protections from successive prosecutions, and ex post facto laws. Liberty is secured in a second way by the constitutional divisions of functions between the states and the federal government and among the three branches at the federal level. The subject of federalism is drawn from the interplay of the grouping of positively assured rights and structural protections, overlaid by assigned roles for the states, the federal government, and the respective branches of the federal government.

Walter Berns in his new book, *Taking the Constitution Seriously*, explains that while great attention has been devoted to the Bill of Rights, grandly asserted by some to be "the very foundation of America's free and democratic society," it was adopted to limit the power of the national government, not the states. Berns reminds us that from 1789 to 1925, the Bill of Rights "played almost no role in the securing of rights. Prior to the *Gitlow* case in 1925, which began the process of incorporation, our absorption of the Bill of Rights into or by the fourteenth amendment (thereby making its provisions applicable to the states), there were few cases involving the first ten amendments and fewer still—in fact, only 15—in which a governmental action was held to be in conflict with one of them. There were only nine such cases during all of the 19th Century, one of these being *Dred Scott v. Sandford* (scarcely a monument to liberty), and another being *Hepburn v. Griswold*, which was promptly overruled."

We must recall that not once during its first 136 years did the Supreme Court strike down an act of Congress on First Amendment grounds; indeed, this did not occur in a speech case until 1965. Nor should we forget that the Bill of Rights has served primarily to limit the acts of state government. This is in no way to demean the great importance of the Bill of Rights. Rather, it is to emphasize that the structural arrangement is also a critical guarantor of liberty— that it has served us well.

Hence, any proposal to expand the lawmaking powers of federal courts in complex cases must account for our constitutional structure. Alteration of this structure is serious business indeed, and sensitivity to the allocation of power among the three branches of federal government and between the federal and state governments requires vigilance.

Role of Courts in Maintaining Structure

A. *Stare decisis*

Gauging the ability of courts to respond to increased complexity requires full appreciation of stare decisis—the central decisional principle for judges. I want to point out here that adherence to precedent must be a key component of our decisional matrix. It limits how far federal courts can and should go in drafting creative responses to the problem of complex litigation.

Merely describing the role of precedent implies a political viewpoint because precedent is inevitably in part, sometimes in large part, in the eye of the beholder. Yet, the concept of precedent is a discipline sufficient to decide the great percentage of cases that come to our court, including constitutional issues. The fact that a little mysticism, priestly role-playing, and postured "discovering" of the law have survived the realists and "law and" supporters, and are still important to the acceptance of judicial lawmaking, does not mean that the concept of precedent lacks content at its core. As Professor David P. Bryden put it in denying that constitutional law is all politics and no law, "[t]he difference between a partial myth and a complete myth is the difference between Abraham Lincoln and the tooth fairy."

As Roger J. Traynor of the California Supreme Court pointed out: "[I]n modern Italian stare means to stay, to stand, to lie, or to sit, to remain, to keep, to stop, or to wait. With delightful flexibility it also means to depend, to fit or to suit, to live and, of course, to be." As we will see, Italian may better describe some views of precedent than the Latin.

The values claimed for precedent are familiar. Professor Wasserstrom lists four major justifications: certainty, reliance, equality, and efficiency. He lists as minor justifications:

> "practical experience, a notion resting upon the hypothesis that judge-made law enables the legal system to adapt itself quite readily to new situations and novel controversies by responding to those situations in a posteriori fashion as they arise; restraint upon the individual judge; and the termination of particular litigation."

There is little to quarrel with here.

As the heartbeat of common law decisionmaking, stare decisis has an important role to play in our decisional matrix. Complex cases will be decided, by and large, under substantive rules of law that have developed through this accretive process. The predictability of these inherited principles itself contributes to the efficient resolution of claims, often without judicial involvement. And, on a deeper level, the pedigree of the legal principle applied justifies and rationalizes the judgments in cases that are litigated. In short, adherence to precedent actuates settled expectations. To the extent the problem of complex litigation requires a departure from this traditional mode of judicial decisionmaking, we must account for its costs.

B. Selection of State Law

The role of stare decisis in our decisional matrix gains further importance in the way it binds over courts on different levels of government. Lawyers and judges have spent much energy attempting to answer the question of what law federal courts are to apply when state interests are implicated. For our purposes, I only remind that when jurisdiction of a federal court rests upon the circumstance that the dispute is between citizens of different states—diversity jurisdiction—the federal court is obligated to apply the law of the state in which it sits. But even this principle has a long and unfinished history.

Congress provided in Section 34 of the Judiciary Act of 1789, the Rules of Decision Act, that:

> "The laws of the several states, except where the Constitution, treaties, or statutes of the United States shall otherwise require or provide, shall be regarded as rules of decision in trials at common law in the court of the United States in cases where they apply."

Professor Charles Alan Wright has observed: "No issue in the whole field of federal jurisprudence has been more difficult than determining the meaning of this statute." (*Law of Federal Courts*, 4th Ed., 1983, p. 347.) The Supreme Court first tried a full answer in 1842 with its decision in *Swift v. Tyson*. (41 U.S. 1 [1842].) Justice Story's opinion for the Court concluded that New York decisions were not the laws of the state under the Rules of Decision Act. For nearly a century, federal courts proceeded to apply their own mix—federal common law—until, in 1938, the Supreme Court overruled its much-criticized *Swift*, concluding that apart from matters governed by the federal Constitution or Acts of Congress, the law to be applied is that of the state. (*Erie Railroad Company v. Tompkins*, 304 U.S. 64 [1938].) Later decisions have since developed the *Erie* rule without putting to rest the debate over whether the requirement that the federal court apply the law of the state is simply a matter of interpreting the statute or whether it is constitutionally mandated. Justice Brandeis's opinion in *Erie* suggested that the rule of *Swift v. Tyson* was "unconstitutional," but the suggestion has only fueled the debate.

Of course, the *Erie* requirement that state law be applied generates a second and related question regarding the source for rules to decide the question of which state's law is to be applied. For example, in a suit brought in a United States District Court in Texas by an Arkansas citizen against a citizen of Texas for an automobile accident occurring in Arkansas, in deciding whether the law of Arkansas or the law of Texas is to be applied, a federal court must draw either upon its own resources, a federal common law, or the law of one of the two states. In 1941, the Supreme Court answered this question in *Klaxon v. Stentor Electric Manufacturing Company, Inc.*, concluding that the federal courts in deciding cases must follow the choice of law rule of the state in which the district court sits. (313 U.S. 487 [1941].) As will be seen, efficient and fair handling of complex cases such as the asbestosis cases requires a close look at the changes in these rules about whose law and at the question of who can make changes.

C. Principles of Preclusion

The recognition given by federal and state courts to the judgments of the other is an important component of federalism and, obviously, of our decisional matrix. As we will see, the doctrine of full faith and credit and the doctrine of issue and claim preclusion not only serve as policies of efficiency and repose but also serve as important implementing tools of our dual system of government. To reduce confusion, I will first explain the horizontal plane of issue and claim preclusion, that is, the preclusive effect upon a second court of an earlier decision by a court located on the same political plane, such as of one federal court upon another. The effect court number two will give presents an identity problem, specifically, the similarity between the two cases, similarity of the parties, and similarity of the issues. Preclusion also turns on the use to be made of the contended for preclusion.

1. Mutuality. Turning to the basics, we first look at the requirement of mutuality. As professor Charles Alan Wright has observed, there are few developments in a judicial principle that are easily traced to one decision and even fewer can be laid to the hand of a single judge. The demise of mutuality is one. Until 1942 the federal courts and virtually all states insisted upon mutuality as a condition to preclusion. Only a party to the earlier case in instances where the other party would also have been bound by the earlier judgment is entitled to preclusion. The bind of the earlier case must have been shared. Justice Traynor's opinion in *Bernhard* held that mutuality was no longer required, that, only "the party against whom the plea . . . is asserted need be a party or in privity with a party to the earlier judgment. (*Bernhard v. Bank of America Nat. Trust & Sav. Ass'n*, 19 Cal.2d 807, 122 P.2d 892, 895 [1941].) Since *Bernhard*, the federal courts supported by the Restatement of Judgments (Restatement [Second] of Judgments 29 [1982]) and most state courts permit some degree of nonmutual issue preclusion. Professor Cassad observes that in recent years only nine states have "reaffirmed their adherence to the Mutuality doctrine."

The relaxation of mutuality has expanded the potential use of a litigated issue in later cases. We have described their uses as offensive or defensive. That is, a defendant can assert that a plaintiff has earlier tried an issue and cannot reargue the issue in the suit against him. A plaintiff can assert that a defendant is precluded from trying a second time an issue decided against the defendant in an earlier case. The Supreme Court has faced both issues.

In *Blonder-Tongue v. University Foundation* (402 U.S. 3123 [1971]), the Court allowed a defendant in a patent infringement case to defend on the basis that the patent had been held invalid in an earlier enforcement effort by the plaintiff, although the defendant had not been a party to the earlier suit. The Court did not insist that the defendant in the second case had been at risk in the first suit, abandoning the requirement of mutuality to that extent. Even so, the Court was cautious, allowing the plaintiff in the second suit to escape its earlier loss on the issue if it demonstrates that the first suit denied a "fair opportunity procedurally, substantively, and evidentially to pursue his claim. . . ."

Patent cases are sufficiently unique that the future of mutuality in other settings was uncertain. But eight years later in *Parklane Hosiery Co. v. Shore* (439 U.S. 322 [1979]), as Professor Resnik put it, "the Court conclusively ended the mutuality of estoppel requirement in the federal courts and authorized the use of nonmutual estoppel." The Court allowed nonmutual offensive use of issue preclusion but in doing so hedged its use in recognition of its distinct opportunities for abuse. Significantly, in my view, the Court rejected the underlying premise of mutuality, that the benefits of an adjudication should be enjoyed only by those who risked an adverse decision. The Court was unwilling to forbid out of the hand the offensive use of prior decrees by strangers. Rather, the Court gave the trial courts considerable discretion to tailor its use to achieve fairness for the defendant. It pointed to four situations where a district court might reject its use: when sought by one who deliberately bypassed an opportunity to participate in the first case that he could easily have joined, when defendant's stake in the earlier case was so small that it lacked proportionate incentives to litigate, where the prior judgment is inconsistent with other judgments, and where the second case offers procedural opportunities not available in the first suit. As Professor Shreve explained, "*Parklane* can best be understood as completing the process, begun in *Blonder-Tongue*, of replacing one fairness test with another."

2. *Claim Definition.* A difference between issue and claim preclusion is that one describes issues actually litigated and the other issues that might have been, but were not litigated. Stated another way,

> "[t]he doctrine of claim preclusion prevents parties to final judgments from relitigating claims and may also foreclose the litigation of new claims. A new claim is precluded when it is so closely related to a previously raised claim that together they constitute a 'claim' in a larger sense. This expanded concept of a claim is intended to signify all of the alternative legal theories and the full scope of remedies generated by the facts of the original controversy. Whether the entire claim, in this broad sense, was actually put forward in the prior case is immaterial; what matters is whether it could have been put forward."

Many of the lower federal courts have subscribed to the transaction approach of the Restatement 24 (1982). Under subsection (1) of the Restatement, the former judgment precludes "all rights of the plaintiff to remedies against the defendant with respect to all or any part of the transaction or series of connected transactions out of which the (original) action arose." Section 2 provides that the scope of the transaction and series of transactions are to be determined pragmatically, giving weight to such considerations as whether the facts are related in time, space, origin, or motivation; whether they form a convenient trial unit; and whether their treatment as a unit conforms to the parties' expectations or business understandings or usage.

From this discussion it is easy to see how issue and claim preclusion can have a powerful effect on the resolution of complex cases. Remember that the hallmark of such cases is that the individual disputes they contain often overlap as to discrete issues of law or fact. An adjudication of the liability of an asbestos manufacturer, for example, to a particular plaintiff may eventually resolve the issue of liability as to all other similarly situated plaintiffs. The only limit to the breadth of the judgment's application, as I explained above, are the four *Parklane* factors.

3. *Full Faith and Credit*. These rules of issue and claim preclusion obviously bind a court to give preclusive effect to its own previous decisions. But the importance of this aspect of the matrix is magnified by the fact that by the Constitution and federal statutes, all other courts, federal and state, must also give preclusive effect to the decision of any particular state or federal court. Article IV, Section I, provides:

> "Full Faith and Credit shall be given in each State to the public Acts Records, and Judicial Proceedings of every other State; And the Congress may by general laws prescribe the Manner in

which such Acts, Records and Proceedings shall be proved, and the Effect thereof."

In 1790, the Congress passed the predecessor to Title 28, Section 1738. Unchanged in any relevant way, the statute now reads:

"The . . . judicial proceedings of any court of any such State . . . shall have the same full faith and credit in every court within the United States and its Territories and Possessions as they have by law or usage in the courts of such State, Territory or Possession from which they are taken."

Doubtlessly, Congress by its 1790 statute gave a vertical reach to the horizontal command of the Constitution, but it is important to remember that this vertical reach is a creature of Congress and is not a constitutional command. It is also important that the obligation of federal courts to give to judgments of state courts the preclusive effect given to them by the rendering state not be confused with their obligations under the Rule of Decision Act to apply state law in diversity cases. For now we can assume that the obligation of federal courts to apply state law in diversity cases has a constitutional base but that Congress is relatively free to alter the deference due state judgments by federal courts. Indeed, some commentators have suggested that, when the state law is uncertain, there is no constitutional impediment to a federal court's application of federal law; that in this respect the statutory command of full faith and credit differs from the obligation to apply state law under the Rule of Decision Act.

D. Consolidation

The extensive overlap of issues in complex cases means that often individual claims of separate parties ought to be adjudicated in consolidated proceedings where the actions have been brought in federal court. Congress has provided the means for transferring cases pending in many different districts to a single district. (See 28 U.S.C. § 1404, et. seq.) The authority to concentrate such cases in one district rests with the Multi-District Litigation Panel, a panel of district court judges.

While transferee districts have considerable power to order trial preparation in ways that reduce duplicative effort, its effectiveness is impaired by two difficulties. First, locating federal cases at a common site may leave pending in the state courts many cases with common issues and many common defendants. Relatedly, while the state and federal cases are under separate management, they are not wholly independent. They remain tied to each other by the doctrine of claim and issue preclusion and by the basic expectation of a rule-ordered society that similar results should be reached in similar cases.

Second, the transfer of federal diversity cases to a single court faces the difficulty that each case comes with the directive to apply the law of the state of the transferee court. (*Van Dusen v. Barrack*, 376 U.S. 612 [1964].) Thus a transferee judge can be asked to apply the law of twenty or thirty states. As I explained, the state law to be applied includes the choice of law rules—that is, which law of several possible will be chosen.

II

With the primary components of our decisional matrix in mind, I now return to the essential question for this paper: what are the most effective ways to manipulate the matrix to accommodate for complex litigation? I will compare two possible alternatives; first, the proposal to create federal common law to govern the rules of decision in such cases; and second, that to give federal courts common-lawmaking power over only the choice-of-law to be applied in complex cases. I suggest that the choice-of-law issues are more issues of state right than of public right and that a federal resolution of disputes between states is consistent with our constitutional vision—that choosing which state law is to be applied is preferable to a federal supplanting of substantive rules.

These inquiries must be made, mindful of the court's duty to abide precedent, to administer a structure that recognizes a rule for the states with distinct power to express policy for its citizens. There are a host of problems. I treat only these issues because my purpose is only to illustrate how the concerns of federalism inform the effort to solve the complexity of this new genre of dispute in ways that are faithful to our sense of due process, access to courts, and fair play for litigants. In the main, my purpose is descriptive, not prescriptive.

The Force of *Klaxon*

I begin with the proposition that *Klaxon v. Stentor Electric Manufacturing Company* (313 U.S. 450 [1941].) was wrongly decided. On one level, of course, the Supreme Court's decision in *Klaxon* seems a logical extension of the rhetoric in *Erie*: federal courts should not be in the business of creating rules of law to apply in diversity cases. The question is whether a federal diversity court may ignore the state's choice-of-law rules any more than it may ignore the substantive legal rules to which they lead.

To begin with, as many commentators have pointed out, a case like *Klaxon* implicates far different concerns of federalism than does a case like *Erie*. The Supreme Court's decision in *Erie* dealt only with the substantive law to be applied to the parties; the only choice-of-law question was whether federal or state rules of decision would govern. By contrast, in *Klaxon* the issue was whether the federal court should apply one state's law or another state's law. Of course, the power to choose between the two itself implicates federalism issues, but the *Klaxon* question primarily involves the horizontal mediation of power *between* states, while the *Erie* question involves the vertical mediation of power between the states and the federal government.

In relying on the force of *Erie*, *Klaxon* ignored the way in which this practical distinction is recognized by our constitutional structure. *Erie* was mandated, in large part, by the fact that federal courts had no enumerated constitutional power to declare the substantive law applicable in what—but for the "accident" of diversity—would be a state-court action. That proposition is unassailable. However, there is a great deal of support in the Constitution's text and history for the notion that federal courts were intended to formulate their own choice-of-law principles for diversity suits.

William Baxter canvassed the evidence in a 1963 law review article. (Choice of Law and the Federal System, 16 Stan. L. Rev. 1 [1963].) He concluded that the drafters of the diversity clause fully expected that federal courts would apply their own choice-of-law rules in diversity cases. After all, the purpose of diversity jurisdiction was to avoid the bias a state court might have for its own citizens. The most effective way for the state court to actuate such a bias would be to favor its own laws when deciding which state's law should apply. Because such bias could infect the state's choice-of-law principles, and not just the application of substantive law, a federal court under *Klaxon* would be no less biased a forum than the state court itself.

This theme recurs, says Professor Baxter, in the language of the Rules of Decision Act, the statute on which *Erie* was built. The Act directs that "the laws of the several states" are to provide the rules of decision in diversity actions, "in cases where they apply," If the states' choice-of-law rules were part of "the laws of the several states"—which is the holding in *Klaxon*—those last five words would not be necessary. Instead, those words might be thought to instruct the federal diversity court to decide, on its own, which state's law applies.

The theory, while not airtight, explains why Justice

Brandeis never considered the choice-of-law problem in *Erie*, and how the Supreme Court in *Sibbach v. Wilson & Co.*, (312 U.S. 1, 10-11 [1941]), six months before *Klaxon*, could assume that a diversity court could make its own choice-of-law decision. The power to create federal choice-of-law rules in diversity was thought as something that survived *Erie*, for it was premised on an entirely different basis than was *Swift v. Tyson*. As Professor Baxter explains,

"Both before and after *Swift* . . . the federal courts exercised independent judgment on choice of law. Choice rules were regarded not merely as general rather than local law but as part of a still more august and transcendent body of principle, the law of nations."

Given this background, the very least we can say is that the result in *Klaxon* was not simply preordained by the Court's reasoning in *Erie*. The constitutional framework, while requiring federal obedience to state substantive law, could have carved out a role for federal diversity courts as the arbiters of conflicts between the laws of the states.

More difficult, however, is whether *Erie's* equal protection concerns are implicated in a *Klaxon* situation. Recall the problem: According to Justice Brandeis, *Swift* was unconstitutional because it gave the nonresident plaintiff a privilege not extended to the resident defendant, a choice between the federal and state rules of decision.

Klaxon might present the same problem. If the

federal court follows a different choice-of-law rule than the courts of the state in which the federal court sits, and if those two rules would result in the selection of different substantive law for the merits of the case, a nonresident plaintiff receives an unconstitutional benefit. But in the view of modern equal protection law, the *Klaxon* situation contains a pivotal difference. An important and rational purpose—the federal court's duty to be the arbiter of conflicts between the laws of several states—justifies unequal treatment.

This analysis is necessarily simplistic. My point, though, is that no serious historical or constitutional principle, aside from respect for precedent, compels the continued application of *Klaxon*. There is room in the decisional matrix to adjust this aspect of adjudicating complex cases.

A World Without *Klaxon*

The question I want to address in more detail is what the world of complex, multiparty litigation would look like in the absence of the *Klaxon* rule. (A similar proposal was made in a recent student note, "Mass Tort Litigation: A Statutory Solution to the Choice of Law Impasse," 96 Yale L.J. 1077 [1987].) The thesis I test is that overruling *Klaxon* would greatly simplify cases like the asbestosis litigation, and would do so in a way far less disruptive to the federal scheme than creation of federal common law for the substantive issues in such cases.

Viewed through the decisional matrix I described in the first part of this paper, the choice-of-law

approach carries significant advantages. Without
Klaxon, the federal court trying a consolidated action
might select the law of one, or perhaps a few, states
and apply it to all the parties. In many cases, this
would greatly simplify the issues and prevent repetitive determinations of law and facts. This I will call
the administratively ideal case.

It is helpful to consider how this process might
work in practice. Imagine a case involving two
manufacturer defendants, one doing business in Texas
and the other in California. The plaintiffs come from
several states, but with a significant concentration in
Utah. For the purpose of choosing which state's law to
apply, the court might group the cases into three
categories: (1) Utah law would apply to those cases involving Utah plaintiffs; (2) Texas law would apply to
those cases involving the Texas defendant but no Utah
plaintiffs; and (3) California law would apply to those
cases involving the California defendant but no Utah
plaintiffs.

Of course, this is a simplified and unlikely example.
Often most or all the plaintiffs in a complex suit will
name the same set of defendant manufacturers, especially where the individual plaintiffs do not know the
identity of the causal defendant. But my point is that
even where the choice-of-law involves complicated
questions of grouping, a world without *Klaxon*
permits the court to consider the efficiencies associated with applying a particular state's law to the controversy.

An important consideration will be issue and claim
preclusion. Remember from the earlier discussion,
the modernized rules of preclusion allow a judgment's

effect to extend beyond the immediate parties, often making repetitive litigation unnecessary. The federal common law approach contains a difficult preclusion problem: what aspects of the federal court's decision, made under federal common law on the merits, can preclude later litigation in state court, where the federal common law would have no application? We can only assume that a state court would not be bound by determinations made under different legal principles. Giving such a judgment preclusive effect would probably be unfair within the *Parklane* framework.

The choice-of-law approach, on the other hand, at least allows the court to preserve the preclusive effect of the federal court's judgment in cases arising later under the state law selected and applied in the diversity action. In fact, it gives the court the power to balance the administrative convenience of applying one state's law against the efficient preclusive effects of applying another state's law. If, in the above example, a great number of cases involving the Texas defendant were left behind in California courts, it might be efficient to group the cases involving the Texas defendant with the cases involving the California defendant and apply California law to both.

Sometimes this will work in reverse: the judge can take into account the preclusive effect of prior state court decisions in determining the choice-of-law issue. In some cases it may be more efficient to apply the law of the state whose courts have already adjudicated cases involving issues or claims now before the federal court.

But beyond these administrative benefits, the chief

advantage of reversing *Klaxon* is that it avoids the disruption of the constitutional balance between the states and federal government. Although the federal courts would have the power to select which state's law to apply, they would not have the power to create federal rules of decision that would displace state rules.

My basic assumption, of course, is that it is better to use rules crafted by states than rules crafted by federal courts. This assumption deserves some explanation. My preference for state rules has two major underpinnings, one practical and one philosophical. On the practical side, I rely on the familiar federalist theme of the experimental capability and flexibility of state governments. There must be truth in the notion that fifty states working on the same problems can collectively generate more refined and intelligent decisional rules than can the relatively concentrated federal court system.

Federally developed rules also might be more intractable. By preserving the states' power to formulate the rules of decision, we also preserve their power to change rules that do not work well. State legislatures often tinker with the common law tort rules developed by state courts. Absent some sort of congressional intervention, a federal common law in these areas would lack such dynamism.

On a broader level, a state rule is also to be preferred because state autonomy is an essential ingredient to the free society that our federalist scheme secures. State governments are structured to inject representativeness into the creation and application of decisional rules. Many states elect their judges. All state legislatures, to some extent, participate in creating and modifying liability rules, statutes of limitations, indemnity rules, and the like. The states' rules of decision to be applied in significant cases such as the asbestosis litigation, then, are the product of legitimate decisionmaking structures sensitive to the local interests such cases affect.

A federal common law governing the rules of decision in complex cases would remove these inputs to the substantive law, replacing it with the wisdom of unelected federal judges. Although federal courts would undoubtedly be sensitive to localized concerns, they need not pay allegiance to the representative values inherent in state common law. In short, the administrative difficulties of complex cases do not necessarily indicate that the legal issues such cases contain have ceased to be localized concerns. This is not an area in which changes in the quality of life make it appropriate to centralize the law-making function.

The federal common law approach would replace these valuable representative inputs with a form of decisionmaking quite unlike traditional common law rulemaking. This is because a federal common law of complex cases would be developed in discrete enclaves. There might be, for example, a federal common law of asbestosis, a federal common law of mass airplane disasters, or a federal common law of toxic wastes. This represents a significant departure from the way in which common law usually develops. As I discussed earlier, when state courts developed the common law principles which would otherwise apply to complex cases, they had to reconcile the needs of particular circumstances with the larger fabric of the law. They had to consider how their decisions fit in with what came before, and how their decision might affect future cases even beyond the circumstantial enclave before them.

It should make us uneasy that a court creating substantive law within these enclaves would be unrestrained by the traditional process of common-lawmaking. A federal court creating the law of airplane disasters need not consider how its rules jibe with broader tort principles, for example. To me, this suggests that a court outside the accretive common law method is, in a very real sense, airborne. If federal courts were constrained to selecting and applying state law in complex cases, the results would be both better and more legitimate.

These are the advantages of a reverse-*Klaxon* approach, but there are disadvantages. Obviously, the federal common law approach is far more potent in an administrative sense. The federal rule of decision would apply in all cases. Even without *Klaxon*, the federal court may find that it cannot apply only one state's law to all the consolidated claims. Indeed, the administratively ideal case is likely to be rare.

Second, I must acknowledge that it seems disingenuous to hope for the administratively ideal result, when the only reason so many cases are consolidated—and thus create multistate choice-of-law issues—is because of a decision of the Multidistrict Litigation Panel. Of course, it may be equally disingenuous to consolidate the cases and then apply federal substantive common law to the claims because the cases have grown too complex.

There is also a sense in which the concerns expressed in our decisional matrix are themselves implicated by the choice-of-law approach. Imagine again the administratively ideal circumstance that a federal court, applying a federal law of conflicts in a case consolidating parties from twenty different states, chooses the law of one state to apply to the entire controversy. In what sense is that really different from the court inventing its own decisional rules, as it would under the federal common law approach? In short, at some point the *selection* of the substantive rules becomes the *creation* of the substantive rules.

Nevertheless, there are two important constraints on the federal court's power within the choice-of-law approach which provide dividing lines between selection and creation. First, a cohesive set of choice-of-law principles exists which no doubt would be the foundation for a federal common law of conflicts. And after some time the discretion of courts will be restrained by prior decisions. Of course, I recognize that the more restrictive the choice-of-law rules, the less likely becomes the administratively ideal case.

More important, though, I suspect that even where conflicts principles permit the federal court to select from a wide variety of rules, the court's power is still far more circumscribed than if it were creating the rules of decision as a matter of federal common law. That is because under the choice-of-law approach, the court will usually have to select the state or states most interested in the controversy and apply the full panoply of decisional rules from that state. In other words, the court cannot take one state's statute of limitations, another state's definition of negligence, and a third state's principles of indemnity. In this sense, the power to select is quite different from the power to create.

In sum, I have tried to compare the choice-of-law approach and the federal common law approaches within the decisional matrix mandated by the federal structure. These considerations behoove us at least to consider a modification to *Klaxon* before we embark upon federal common-lawmaking for the rules of decision in complex cases.

Implementation

If we were to agree that overruling *Klaxon* would be both beneficial and constitutionally sound, we would still have to decide how the job would best be done, by the Supreme Court or by legislative enactment. That choice itself implicates the concerns of our decisional matrix. A congressional enactment would eliminate the need for the Supreme Court to overrule itself, and a statutory change might be easier to modify if it proved ineffective. And assuming there is still value in the *Klaxon* rule for most cases, a statutory change could be more narrowly tailored. Perhaps *Klaxon* would only be overruled for the purposes of certain categories of complex cases.

It is also worth considering how our earlier discussion of the recent decision in *Garcia v. San Antonio Metropolitan Transit Authority* (469 U.S. 538, 105 S.Ct. 1005 [1985]) bears on the power of congress to implement some sort of reverse-*Klaxon* rule. In *Garcia* the Court held that Congress's power to interfere with "core" state functions is limited only by the structural arrangement of our federal system; courts will not review such actions. Obviously, even assuming choice-of-law is a "core" government function of the states, the current majority position poses no barrier to reverse *Klaxon*. Under the current law courts are not to consider challenges to federal regulation of a state's "core" activities with any more scrutiny than it would regulation of a private individual's activity. Even assuming the application of choice-of-law rules is a "core" state activity, the interstate nature of cases like the asbestosis litigation would certainly provide footing for federal legislation.

But we should consider whether the minority in *Garcia*, poised as it is to reverse the decision, would permit a federal choice-of-law statute. I doubt there would be much difficulty. The minority position advocates a test balancing the state's interest in its activity against the federal interest, the latter here being quite strong. This is especially true given the historical background of the diversity clause; a federal choice-of-law statute could be considered necessary and proper to implement that provision.

III

All courts are now facing a new genre of lawsuits that challenge basic assumptions behind present litigation models. I have painted with a broad brush. Each of the issues discussed is worthy of extended examination, including the question of whether we should abandon the present use of state choice-of-law rules by federal courts. My mission here is narrow in purpose despite the broad description of subject. I hope to remind that the problems attending the growing complexity of our society and its disputes must be faced with the basic principle of federalism in mind; that concern for efficiency must accommodate the Constitution's deliberate dispersal of power, a calculated use of inefficiency that recognized the corrupting force of unchecked power and men's unchanging janus-faced capacity for both good and evil.

DEFAMATION:
A TALE OF TWO COUNTRIES

by

George A. Birrell

George A. Birrell

George A. Birrell, Esq., has been counsel to the New York law firm of Dorsey & Whitney since May 1986. Prior to this, he was the General Counsel of the publicly-held parent company in the Mobil group for 16 years. He also served as a Director and Vice President of Mobil Corporation.

Before joining Mobil in 1958, Mr. Birrell was a member of the firm of Donovan Leisure Newton & Irvine. He earned both his undergraduate and law degrees from Yale University.

Mr. Birrell is a fellow of the American Bar Foundation, a member and past president of the Association of General Counsel, and a member of the American Law Institute. He served the Department of State as a member of the advisory commission on the Law of the Sea, and has served The Southwestern Legal Foundation as a member of the Advisory Boards of its International and Comparative Law Center and International Oil and Gas Educational Center. Also active in civic affairs, Mr. Birrell served on various commissions and boards and as a member of the city council of Rye, New York, of which he was acting mayor 1970-72. He is a veteran of World War II, having served in the U.S. Army Air Force.

DEFAMATION: A TALE OF TWO COUNTRIES

by

George A. Birrell

"The right of a man to the protection of his own reputation from unjustified invasion and wrongful hurt reflects no more than our basic concept of the essential dignity and worth of every human being—a concept at the root of any decent system of ordered liberty." (*Rosenblatt v. Baer*, 383 U.S. 75, 92, 86 S.Ct. 669, 679 [1966].)

Although these words were written in a concurring opinion in 1966 by Supreme Court Justice Potter Stewart, the concept, so essential to democracy, is not a modern one. At the turn of this century legal historian Van Vechten Veeder had this to say of the historic tension between protection of reputation and freedom of expression, two of the most important moral values in a free society:

"If the laws of each age were formulated systematically, no part of the legal system would be more instructive than the law relating to defamation. Since the law of defamation professes to protect personal character and public institutions from destructive attacks, without sacrificing freedom of thought and the benefit of public discussion, the

135

estimate formed of the relative importance of these objects and the degree of success attained in reconciling them, would be an admirable measure of the culture, liberality, and practical ability of each age." (Veeder, *The History and Theory of the Law of Defamation*, 3 Col. L. Rev. 546, 546 [1903].)

Veeder would have been at least fascinated by the events of the last two decades in the United States and England, and, by that measure, perhaps disappointed in the United States, because it has achieved a reconciliation of these conflicting values that is satisfactory to no one.

In 1964, the two great democracies of the Western world parted company on the issue of the manner of harmonization of the conflicting values of freedom of speech and security of reputation. After sharing with England a common heritage and developing in parallel a common balancing point between these conflicting values over a century and a half, the United States in 1964 decided to abandon the historically developed point of equilibrium, and, ostensibly, to weight the scales sharply in favor of the press. England, on the other hand, considered, and specifically rejected, this departure from the traditional balance.

According to Justice Black, concurring in the landmark *New York Times Company v. Sullivan*:

"To punish the exercise of [a] . . . right to discuss public affairs or to penalize it through libel judgments is to abridge or shut off discussion of the very kind most needed. This Nation, I suspect, can live in peace without libel suits based on public discussions of public affairs and public officials. But *I doubt that a country can live in freedom where its people can be made to suffer . . . financially for criticising their government, its actions, or its officials . . .* An unconditional right to say what one pleases about public affairs is what I consider to be the minimum guarantee of the First Amendment." (376 U.S. 254, 297, 84 S.Ct. 710, 735 [1964].)

In a later concurring opinion, Justice Black added:

"[I]n my view, the First Amendment does not permit the recovery of libel judgments against the news media even when statements are broadcast with knowledge they are false. . . . [I]t is time for this Court to . . . adopt the rule to the effect that the First Amendment was intended to leave the press free from the harassment of libel judgments." (*Rosenbloom v. Metromedia, Inc.*, 403 U.S. 29, 57, 91 S.Ct. 1811, 1826-27 [1971].)

An English Parliamentary Committee appointed to study and recommend changes in the English law of defamation in 1975 rejected this view in these words: "[W]e feel that carte blanche to the press would be intolerable." (*Report of the Committee on Defamation*, 1975, CMND. 5909, p. 168 [hereinafter "Faulks Committee"].)

The Court's opinion in *Sullivan*, of course, stopped short of Black's imperative for a free society. In order to insure "that debate on public issues should be uninhibited, robust and wide-open . . ." (376 U.S. 254, 270, 84 S.Ct. 710, 721), however, the Court established a new rule according immunity to the media in defamation cases brought by public officials except where a plaintiff could prove deliberate falsification or reckless disregard for truth or falsity. This *Sullivan* rule has been embraced by the media in the United States as an essential.but unsatisfactory minimum protection for them. Their position, as reflected in briefs in a recent Supreme Court case, is that their First Amendment rights are so fundamental that the interest of the individual in protecting his reputation must yield whenever it conflicts with those rights. (Surkin, *The Status of the Private Figure's Right to Protect His Reputation Under the United States Constitution*, 90 Dick. L. Rev. 667, 688 n. 5 [1986].)

The Faulks Committee also considered the wisdom of this less draconian measure and rejected it in these words: "No English witness who gave evidence before us advocated the adoption of this new American principle in this country. We oppose it most strongly because we believe that here it would in many cases deny a just remedy to defamed persons." (Faulks Committee, p. 169.) The English witnesses included representatives of every major English media enterprise.

How could two societies, each so firmly dedicated to the protection of individual human rights, reach such different conclusions regarding the optimum formula for harmonizing freedom of speech and security of reputation? Are the media in England shackled and inhibited by self-censorship induced by defamation liability to the point where they are inadequately performing their function? Do the media in the United States really need a rule of law which, in the words of Justice Potter Stewart, "ultimately protects . . . defamatory falsehood" in order to survive and perform their function? (*Rosenblatt v. Baer*, 383 U.S. 75, 92, 86 S.Ct. 669, 679 [1966].)

Security of Reputation, An Ancient Right

Historically, defamation has long been regarded as a wrong for which redress should be accorded. Mosaic, Greek, and Roman law all recognized defamation as a wrong. Security of reputation as a concept long antedates the modern concept of freedom of expression. Indeed, the Old Testament Book of Leviticus records a prohibition on "talebearing" as one of the "miscellaneous ordinances" given by God to Moses. (Veeder, p. 548; Carr, *The English Law of Defamation*, 18 L. Q. Rev. 255, 256 [1902]; Leviticus 19:16 ["Thou shalt not go up and down as a tale bearer among thy people"].)

It is somewhat surprising to be made aware occasionally that litigation is not a new phenomenon. One historian has written of ancient Rome that from "the reign of one emperor to another, litigation was a rising tide which nothing could stem, throwing on the public courts more work than men could muster. To mitigate the congestion of the courts Augustus, as early as the year 2 B.C., was obliged to resign to their use the forum he had built and which bears his name." (J. Carcopino, *Daily Life in Ancient Rome*, 1940, pp. 186-187.) This litigation no doubt included

defamation disputes, for Roman law was much concerned with defamation. As I shall point out, it has
had a profound influence on the law of defamation,
particularly in civil law countries, (Veeder, p. 548,
n. 1.) but to a lesser extent on England and its cultural
child, the United States.

Roman law dealt extensively with defamation. In
early Roman law, verbal injuries were treated as
criminal. The essence of the injury was the personal
insult for which there had to be atonement, a vindic-
tive remedy which took the place of personal
revenge. The most common form of defamatory
material was the libelous chant or song, which at that
time was the form of defamation which secured widest
publication and, therefore, greatest impact. The
milder form of these actions fell under the civil wrong
category known as "injuria," which covered every
form of personal aggression whether accompanied by
force or not. (*Id.*, pp. 563-564.)

Later Roman jurisprudence divided verbal injuries
into two categories, one consisting of defamatory
statements made in a public manner and the other of
such statements made in private. The essence of the
former as an offense was the unjustifiable contumely
offered to the person insulted. Truth was not a
defense because it did not justify the public manner
in which the statements were made. The latter, on the
other hand, permitted truth as a defense. A civil action (known as *actio aestimatio*) lay for a money
penalty which was based on the gravity of the charge
and included, but was not limited by, compensatory
damages.

Subsequently, Roman law established severe

criminal penalties for certain kinds of defamation known as "libelli famosi." These included epigrams and "pasquinades," the latter being the name given to a statue in Rome on which lampoons were posted. By their nature these were anonymous and scurrilous and were visited with severe punishment whether true or false. Again it was the unnecessarily public and offensive manner of publication which was regarded as precluding justification. (*Id.*, p. 564.)

Thus we see in Roman law a distinction based on manner and extent of publication, but, unlike the later common law, with no distinction between written and oral delivery. It is clear that the element of bad motive or malice or, stated another way, lack of justification made a large difference in the remedy available. It is also a reflection of the policy of Roman law not to protect bad reputation or prevent appropriate discussion of that reputation.

The beginnings of the law of defamation among the Germanic peoples goes back to very early times. The blood feud remedy was gradually replaced by the *wer*, a money payment as compensation for injury. This applied to defamation. (*Id.*, p. 548.) The *Lex Salica*, the most ancient of the barbarian codes dating from the fifth century A.D. and attributed to the Salic Franks (*Black's Law Dictionary*, 4th ed., 1968, p. 1505), provided that if one calls a man a "wolf" or a "hare" he must pay three shillings; for a false imputation of unchastity against a woman, the fine was forty-five shillings. By the terms of the *Norman Costumal*, if one falsely called another "thief" or "manslayer" he had to pay damages, and publicly confess himself a liar. The theory of these remedies was that they were compensation to the wronged individual for the surrender of his older right of private vengeance, and the penalty, thus, tended to equate with the degree of irritation expected. (Veeder, pp. 548-549.) In early Icelandic law, the man accused of cowardice had the right to slay his accuser.

The importance of reputation in those times is, perhaps, better understood when it is remembered that good reputation was a defense to almost every crime.

Origins of Defamation in England

In England, Alfred the Great, King of the West Saxons from 871 to 901, perhaps in his *Dombec* which is now lost, established the rule that a slanderer should have his tongue cut out unless he could redeem it with the price of his head. English laws exacted *bot* (compensation) or *wite* (penalty) from those who gave bad names. Pleadings in this period in the local courts indicate a prevailing sensitivity to dishonor or disgrace. In a case of physical beating, the award would separately cover the dishonor element. (Veeder, p. 549.)

In the thirteenth and fourteenth centuries, actions were common in the local (seignorial or manorial) courts. In these local courts, reputation could be cleared before the people to whom the defamation was originally published. One result of the apparent effectiveness of this local remedy was that, even when King's Courts later first became established, there seem to have been no actions for defamation. This, however, had changed by the end of the sixteenth century when the manorial courts were in decay.

In the light of the later development of the law of libel and slander in the more exalted King's Courts, it is interesting to note the sensitivity of the manorial courts to all forms of slander. One commentator cites thirteenth century records indicating damages given for calling another a "false man, full of frauds, and a picker of quarrels" and in another case for one woman calling another "a sorceress and a liar." (Carr, *The English Law of Defamation*, 18 L.Q. Rev. 255, 265-266 [1902].) Under the law of defamation as it was subsequently formulated in the King's Courts, none of these slanders would have prompted redress absent proof of special damages. In fact, one is struck by the fact that the later development of the law of defamation in the King's Courts, which became the only law of defamation in modern England, seems to have been little influenced by doctrines relating to slander or spoken defamation developed in the manorial courts.

Meanwhile, another force was at work. In the Middle Ages, the Church achieved success in establishing its own jurisdiction over many aspects of secular life. It developed its own tribunals, its own procedures, and its own practitioners.

The Churches claimed jurisdiction not just over what we would regard as religious matters but also over matrimonial and testamentary matters. Its broadest claim was jurisdiction to correct the sinner for his soul's health. Under this heading came sexual morality, usury, perjury, and defamation. The Church

took over the Roman Law concept of "injuria," technically meaning insult but carrying a much broader
meaning in the sense that insult could come in many
forms including direct force and verbal abuse. A
physical blow could be an affront to one's dignity.
These injuries as a class became, in ecclesiastical law,
"diffimation." The Church, responsible for upholding
virtue in men's lives, stayed the tongue of the
defamer. The typical penance exacted was an
acknowledgment of the falseness of the charge before
the officials of the Church, and an apology to the
person defamed.

Meanwhile, another momentous event had
occurred. Starting in 1275, with the Statute of
Westminster the First in the reign of Edward I, a
series of laws were enacted which became known as
"*Scandalum Magnatum.*" These created a statutory
offense of defamation under which it was illegal to
spread either spoken or written "false news" or tales
concerning the king or the magnates of the realm.
(Hamburger, *The Development of the Law of
Seditious Libel and the Control of the Press*, 37 Stan.
L. Rev. 661, 668 [1985].) This was one of the first
efforts of the crown in England to devise a rifle shot
legal remedy for disruptive criticism. It provided a
basis for both criminal and civil actions, but it was, of
course, of no use to the ordinary common man. It was
of limited use even to the crown and the great men of
the realm because it applied only to "news," and truth
may have been a defense. "*Scandalum Magnatum*"
continued to be refined in the reigns of Richard II
(1378), Bloody Mary (1554), and Elizabeth I (1559),
and is one of the antecedents of seditious libel.

The King's Courts in the period prior to the reign of Elizabeth did not entertain pleas of defamation. This was, in part at least, due to the claim of the ecclesiastical courts to exclusive jurisdiction in this area, and in part due to the availability of a remedy in the lesser courts of the realm. By Elizabeth's time, this seems to have changed. Commencing in the reign of Elizabeth I, and growing in those of James I and Charles I, many such actions were entertained in which rules of liability were formulated without regard to form of publication, but came later to be applied exclusively to oral defamation.

The process by which only certain insults came in this period to be regarded as actionable in the King's Courts is not clear. It may have been a combination of distaste for the action, the technical justification used for assuming jurisdiction, and a reluctance to circumscribe permitted speech. The result was that only three categories of speech would support an action without more: Imputations of an indictable offense or crime, inputations of having certain contagious disorders, e.g., syphilis, leprosy, and the plague, and imputation affecting a man's reputation for skill in his business, office, trade, profession, or occupation which tended to prejudice him. One other category allowed an action for any imputation which, in fact, caused special damage.

One commentator believes that this selection of basis for action is attributable directly to the technical basis relied upon for the assumption of jurisdiction. It was an established principle of law at that time that jurisdiction over a thing carried with it jurisdiction over all things accessory. Jurisdiction over crimes might carry with it the authority to investigate the truth of the complainant's charge, and, if false, to provide a remedy to the injured party. Thus, the conclusion was that the label "thief" was actionable while the label "thievish knave" was not. In the latter case, there is not the imputation of an actual crime, only a tendency. So with leprosy and the plague, for those afflicted were subject to commitment to pest houses. Syphilis may have fallen in the same category because of the similarity of its later symptoms to leprosy. Words relating to certain officials, such as attorneys, relate to the administration of justice; assertions of incompetent business or professional abilities relate to bankruptcy, a matter well within the Court's jurisdiction.

One other element was a factor in this explosion of defamation litigation. The "code of honor" under which men had for centuries avenged themselves by dueling was falling into both official and unofficial disrepute, the former because it was perceived as a threat to public peace. Thus the restraint imposed by the "code of honor" may have been disappearing.

In this period, another event of momentous importance to the law of defamation occurred. In 1476, Caxton had set up his printing press at Westminster, and the art spread rapidly in the next hundred years.

The Church had had a long history of suppression of pernicious ideas and the books that embodied them. Secular authority cooperated by burning prohibited works. The advent of the printing press made this no longer effective, and, instead, the Church attempted to prevent the printing of prohibited works. In England, censorship of the press passed with ecclesiastical supremacy to the Crown early in the sixteenth century. The English Catholic Church had, since the early 1400s, asserted the right to control printing through licensing. King Henry VIII in 1538 transferred this authority to the Star Chamber, originally a court of criminal jurisdiction. Its powers were extended by Henry VIII to the point where there were practically no limits.

Later, as the seventeenth century progressed, press censorship through existing legal tools (treason, *Scandalatum Magnatum*, licensing, heresy, etc.) became inadequate to cope with the rising tide of political tracts which were achieving wide circulation in the country. This new and alarming form of scandal cried for a new remedy, and the Star Chamber, with its unlimited jurisdiction, finally devised one in a 1605 case which is known as *De Libellis Famosis*, reported by Lord Coke.

Coke, Attorney General at that time, prosecuted one Lewis Pickeringe for a violation of law which Coke referred to as "libel of magistrates." Pickeringe had written and given to a friend a defamatory rhyme about the then recently deceased Archbishop of Canterbury, Whitgift. It was alleged that it was "against" the dear bishop, the dead Queen, and the dead bishop's successor, and, "by implication against our King." Pickeringe, among other things, denied that it was libelous, and said that, in any event the bishop was dead. (Hamburger, pp. 693-695; Veeder, pp. 563-566.)

As existing law was inadequate, including that developing in the King's Courts, the Star Chamber turned to Roman Law and imported the concept of *libelli famosi* into a newly defined wrong, but in modified form. The libel against a private person incites the individual and all his kin to revenge and breach of the peace. The libel against a magistrate or other public person is a greater offense because it concerns not only a breach of the peace but also the scandal of government, "for what greater scandal of government can there be than to have corrupt or wicked magistrates to be appointed and constituted by the king to govern his subjects?" Truth or falsity was immaterial because publication tends in any event to disturb a "settled state of government," and it "robs a man of his good name, which ought to be more precious than his life." (Veeder, p. 565.)

This was the beginning of the English law of libel. It was aimed at printing, but it covered any writing as well. It was both criminal and civil. Unlike the Roman model, it was not aimed only at the unsigned pasquinade. It articulated as its rationale the potential for breach of the peace rather than simply the unjustified damage to the target's honor and reputation. In the still politically unstable seventeenth century, this may well have been a valid consideration.

This landmark decision had profound implications for the law of defamation. It was the blueprint for the implement upon which the government came more and more to rely in the closing years of the seventeenth century to continue its control of written dissent. The Star Chamber was abolished in 1640. Licensing laws, although renewed thereafter from time to time, expired or became less effective and

completely expired by 1695. For the reasons
mentioned before, *Scandalum Magnatum* was ineffective in many cases, particularly where manuscripts
were involved. Treason carried punishment perceived as too serious to fit the crime, and it required
proof of intent to do bodily harm to the king or to
overthrow the government. This pushed criminal
libel to the fore in cases where magistrates or other
government officials were the objects of verbal attack.
One commentator counts eighteen prosecutions for
seditious libel in the seventeenth century before
1696, of which six cases involved prosecution of libels
which defamed private persons. (Hamburger, p. 763.)

On the civil side, it pointed the way to the creation
in the late seventeenth century of the civil remedy for
a libel. This occurred in 1670 in a case styled *King v.
Lake*, which created a new tort: written defamation.
King, a barrister, claimed Lake's petition to Parliament was "stuffed with illegal assertions" which injured his good name. Lord Chief Baron Hale held
that, although such words spoken once without writing would not be actionable, since they were in writing and published "which contains more malice than
if they had been once spoken, they [were] actionable." (Veeder, p. 570.)

The matter, then, of the civil action for defamation
in the King's Courts and the distinction between
written and oral offenses were, thus, clearly articulated. With a case called *Thorley v. Lord Kerry* in
1812, this distinction became irrevocably embedded
in the common law. Sir James Mansfield, in deliver-
ing the judgment of the Court, acknowledged that a

distinction had existed between written and spoken slander for 150 years and that it was too late to change.

Thus, by the beginning of the nineteenth century, the modern outlines of actionable defamation had evolved. Written defamation is libel; spoken defamation is slander. Libel is a crime as well as a tort. Slander of a private individual may be a tort, but it is no crime. Any written words which injure one's reputation are libelous, but many words which would be actionable if written are not actionable if spoken. In the case of slander, to be actionable, the words used must impute the commission of a crime or the presence of certain contagious disorders, or they must disparage the office, profession, or trade of the complainant. In all other cases, mere spoken words, to be actionable, must have caused some pecuniary loss.

This lengthy history of the evolution of the law of defamation has been pursued because it is instructive as to the importance civilization has historically attached to protection of reputation. This is not a modern notion, nor a product of the industrial revolution. Rather it is as old as civilization, as important a right as the right to protection of person or property. As the law of torts evolved to provide security to individuals, it encompassed not only security to person and property but, of equal importance, to reputation as well. This is illustrated by the Pennsylvania Declaration of Rights of 1790:

"Section I . . .
"All men are born equally free and independent

and have certain inherent and indefeasible rights, among which are those of enjoying and defending life and liberty, *of acquiring, possessing, and protecting property and reputation.* . . . (Emphasis added.)

"Section II . . .
"All courts shall be open; and every man for any injury done him in his lands, *goods, person, or reputation shall have remedy by due course of law.* . . . (Surkin, pp. 671-672. Emphasis added.)

As one Australian commentator put it, "A reputation is a man's most highly prized treasure, hard to win and easy to lose" (Paton, *Reform and the English Law of Defamation*, 33 Ill. L. Rev. NW. U. 669, 669 [1939]), and Shakespeare neatly pointed out a difference between theft of property and theft of reputation, a difference which makes the latter less justifiable:

"Who steals my purse steals trash; 'tis something, nothing;
'Twas mine, 'tis his, and has been slave to thousands;
But he that filches my good name
Robs me of that which not enriches him
And makes me poor indeed." (*Othello*, Act III, Sc. 3.)

An understanding of this historical development of the law of defamation would seem significant to an understanding and evaluation of the developments of

the nineteenth and twentieth centuries in England
and the United States.

The United States and England in the Pre-Sullivan Modern Era

Until the middle of the twentieth century, the civil
law of defamation in those two countries, broadly
speaking, evolved in parallel ways, and was, in fact,
closely interrelated. Thanks in part to colonial status,
cultural heritage, and to Sir William Blackstone's
"Commentaries on the Laws of England," published
in 1765 and 1769, the English common law became
the law of the new Republic, and has, of course, continued so in modified form to this day. Blackstone had
a profound influence on law in the United States in
the early years because his treatise was the only
comprehensive source readily available, there then
being no systematic collection and publication of
court decisions. To the extent such reports existed,
collection represented an expense which few could
afford.

In the United States, the law of defamation was a
matter left to the states. Except for a brief excursion
into the field of criminal libel in the early days of the
republic, neither the Congress nor the federal courts
played any part in the development of the law of libel
and slander until well into the twentieth century.
Although the eventually 50 states produced sometimes differing rules in this field, the general trend
was cohesive and on the major substantive rules there
was considerable uniformity.

In both countries, defamation law stayed within the

basic framework which had evolved at the beginning of the nineteenth century. The distinction between libel and slander, although widely condemned, persisted. Written defamation could be actionable, whatever it was, if it tended to hold the plaintiff up to hatred, contempt, or ridicule, or to cause him to be shunned or avoided. (*Prosser and Keeton on Torts*, W. Keeton ed., 5th ed., 1984, p. 773.) Oral defamation, on the other hand, was only actionable without proof of actual damages if it imputed a crime, a loathsome disease, or incompetence in the plaintiff's business, trade, or profession. (*Id.*, p. 788.)

One resulting anomaly was that defamation relating to female chastity was actionable if written but not if spoken. This was corrected in England by the Slander of Women Act in 1891. Similarly, in the United States, statutory changes to the same effect have been made in many states and in most others the common law rule has been changed by court decision to accord women equal protection.

Modern forms of communication have caused problems. In England, a 1934 court decision held talking pictures to be libel, and, by a 1952 statute, all forms of wireless communication, i.e., radio and television, were classified as libel. (Faulks Committee, p. 93.) In the United States, the result is the same for motion pictures but there is still no settled rule as to whether radio and television broadcasts should be classified as libel or slander. (Prosser, pp. 786-787.)

The question of the standard by which defamation was to be judged produced a divergence. In England it was held that printed matters must tend to defame the individual in the eyes of the community in general, rather than in the opinion of any particular group or class. In the United States the rule is different. It is recognized that a person may be harmed if he is lowered in the esteem of any substantial and respectable group, even though a minority one. Thus, the publication of a picture of the plaintiff in connection with a whiskey advertisement was held actionable in the United States. (*Peck v. Tribune Co.*, 214 U.S. 185, 29 S.Ct. 555 [1909].)

In both England and the United States, strict liability for libel and for slander which is actionable per se continued to be applied. Once defamation was established, damage and falsity were presumed. In the United States, the damage presumed (called "general damages") was the jury's assessment of what was appropriate for the injury to the plaintiff's reputation, his wounded feelings, humiliation, and resulting physical pain or illness as well as future damages of the same kind. (Prosser, pp. 794-795.) The special damages necessary to make oral defamation actionable, however, were limited to damages of a pecuniary nature. Once actual pecuniary loss was proved, however, general damages could also be recovered.

In England, similarly, damage presumed was to be quantified by the jury as the amount necessary to compensate the plaintiff for the damage to his reputation, for the injury to his pride and personal feelings, taking into account aggravation of such injury where there may have been high handed or contumelious conduct. (Faulks Committee, pp. 93-95.)

In both countries, punitive or exemplary damages

were available, that is, damages intended to punish the defendant as distinguished from compensating the plaintiff. In the United States, prior to *New York Times v. Sullivan* and its progeny, these were awarded in defamation cases generally under the same standards applied to other types of action under applicable state law. In England prior to 1964, there was considerable confusion in defamation cases as to what was "punitive" and what was included in the "aggravated compensatory" component of ordinary damages which juries were to award for the injury to pride and personal feelings taking into account contumelious conduct.

Then as a result of the decision in *Rookes v. Barnard* (1964), punitive damages generally were severely limited in England. The new rule left only one narrow ground for punitive damages in defamation cases. Lord Devlin laid it down that punitive damages should only be available in cases involving:

> "Oppressive, arbitrary, or unconstitutional conduct by government officials;
> Conduct calculated to make more money for defendant than the damages otherwise payable to the plaintiff;
> Specific statutory authorization."

Thus only where proof could be made that a defendant published defamatory matter somehow calculating that he would make more than the damage he would be called upon to pay would punitive damages be available in a defamation case.

In the United States, a *Sullivan* offspring, *Gertz v.*

Welch (418 U.S. at 323) in 1974 made punitive damages recoverable only on proof of "First Amendment malice," that is, proof by a plaintiff that the defamatory matter was published either with knowledge that it was false or with reckless disregard for whether it was false or not.

Strict liability also came to mean that intention and malice (in its conventional as opposed to its first amendment sense) were irrelevant. At an earlier time in England a different view prevailed, perhaps as a carryover from church jurisdiction. Malice was a necessary ingredient of the cause of action. In 1825, however, it was held in England that "malice" would be inferred as a matter of law from publication of defamatory material even though the defendant bore plaintiff no ill will and honestly believed what he said was true. This was carried to its logical conclusion in a case decided in 1910 styled *Hulton v. Jones*. The defendants published a newspaper story, sent to them by their Paris correspondent, that a person they believed to be fictitious, one Artemus Jones, had been seen in Dieppe with a woman not his wife. A real Artemus Jones materialized from North Wales, claiming that his neighbors had understood the story to refer to him. The House of Lords affirmed a decision in Jones' favor and 1750 pounds in damages, holding that the defendant's innocence was no defense. (Prosser, p. 808.) The same rule was adopted in the United States. If a defamatory meaning which was false was reasonably understood, the defendant published at his peril.

Paralleling the entrenchment of strict liability was the clearer definition and development of certain

absolute and qualified privileges. The publication of
defamation in furtherance of certain public and
private interests was immune from suit. Absolute immunity meant that purpose, motive, or reasonable-
ness of conduct was irrelevant. There was no liability.
Absolute privilege was and is accorded in both countries to judicial proceedings, legislative proceedings,
proceedings of executive officers charged with
responsibility of importance, publications made with
the consent of the plaintiff, and communications
between husband and wife. (*Id.*, pp. 815-816.)

With respect to judicial proceedings, the immunity
extends to utterances by judges, attorneys, parties,
witnesses, and jurors, and, in England, it covers any
utterance arising out of the proceeding and having
any reasonable relation to it. In the United States, the
rule seems to be more limited. The statement must
have some relation or reference to the subject of inquiry, a rule liberally construed in favor of the defendant. But entirely extraneous statements would not
be protected.

Immunity for members of legislative bodies was
established in England in the seventeenth century
and covered any acts in the performance of their
duties by the members of the legislature, provided
that the defamation had some relation to the business
of the legislature. (*Id.*, pp. 820-821.) In the United
States, by constitutional provision, the protection extends to anything whatever which is said in the course
of the legislative proceedings themselves. In neither
country is absolute privilege extended to republica-
tion outside the legislature. With respect to the
proceedings of government executives, it is not clear

how far down the line the absolute privilege may go.

Qualified privileges have been extended to publication of defamation in certain situations, provided publication is made in a reasonable manner for a proper purpose. One English judge defined the qualified privilege as a publication "fairly made by a person in discharge of some public or private duty, whether legal or moral, or in the conduct of his own affairs in matters where his interest is concerned." (*Id.*, pp. 824-825.) Examples are statements in defense of one's own reputation when threatened by another's defamation, warning a woman that the person she is about to marry is an ex-convict, or warning a business associate of the threatened bankruptcy of a customer.

A qualified privilege of importance to this paper is that known as "fair comment." In order to promote and protect the privilege of free discussion of matters of public interest, the qualified privilege of "fair comment" developed. Under English law this covered expressions of opinion (as distinguished from statements of fact) on any matter of public interest, provided that the facts alleged, if any, were true, the expression of opinion was such that an honest man holding strong exaggerated or even prejudiced views could have held it, the subject matter was of public interest, and the facts relied upon were in the defendant's mind when he made the comment. If the statement contained defamatory statement of fact the defense of fair comment would not apply to those statements. (Faulks Committee, p. 38.)

Where there was an imputation of dishonorable or corrupt motives, restrictions were placed on the defense. The motive imputed could be treated as a statement of fact and thus fall outside the privilege. Difficulties arose in cases in which defamatory facts were stated and defamatory motives imputed from those facts.

The formulation of this qualified privilege in the United States was generally in line with English law. A qualified privilege also developed in favor of reports of official proceedings. In the United States this extended to all legislative and court proceedings and to the quasi-judicial actions of officials of national, state, and municipal governments. This was based on the obvious importance of the public's interest in such events. It covered proceedings of private groups, such as a stockholders' meeting, if open to the public and clearly dealing with matters of public interest. (Prosser, pp. 836-838.)

English law was similar with respect to judicial and legislative proceedings. although there is authority that the privilege relating to reports of judicial proceedings was absolute. This resulted from an ambiguity in the Law of Libel Amendment Act of 1888 (as varied by Sections 8 and 9 of the Defamation Act of 1952) which provides that fair and accurate reports in newspapers or on radio or television of judicial proceedings in the United Kingdom if published contemporaneously are "privileged" without specifying whether absolute or qualified status was intended. Based on *Hansard*, the official report of Parliamentary proceedings, Parliament intended a qualified privilege. (Faulks Committee, p. 48.)

Beyond judicial and parliamentary proceedings, qualified privilege in England has become regulated by statute. It is not clear whether it extends to the same degree as in the United States to reports of inferior governmental bodies such as municipal councils and quasi-judicial actions of state and local officials.

The defense of qualified privilege is only available under both English and United States law if it is exercised in a reasonable manner and for a proper purpose. The principal ground for denial of the privilege is publication with the wrong state of mind. If the principal purpose is, for example, to injure the plaintiff, then the privilege is lost. This has historically been referred to as "malice." But more than ill will toward the plaintiff is required. It must be established that the purpose was not primarily furthering an interest which is entitled to protection.

Truth has historically been a complete defense in civil actions for defamation in England at least since the beginning of the eighteenth century. The contrary rule applied in cases of criminal libel was never imported into the civil action. Perhaps the reason was that public policy demanded that the truth not be fettered by fear of damage suits. This is also the predominant rule in the United States. It is irrelevant that the facts were published for no good reason, out of spite, or even that the publisher did not believe them to be true when published. This has been criticized in some quarters, and a few states have enacted statutory provisions requiring that publication must have been for good motives or justifiable ends. One has reached the same conclusion by court decision without benefit of statutory change of the common law. A 1969 Illinois court decision held that a statute of this type was unconstitutional as a violation of the freedom of the press provision of the First Amendment. Whether there is anything left of the limitation on the defense of truth in the United States is, thus, questionable at best. (Prosser, p. 841.)

Criminal Libel

Meanwhile, the law of criminal libel, so prominent as a means for dealing with criticism of government officials in the seventeenth and eighteenth centuries, went into eclipse as a means of dealing with sedition. In England this decline in efficacy was reflected in certain significant changes in the law. The Libel Act of 1792 provided that "libel or no libel" is henceforth a question for the jury. The Libel Act of 1843 (Lord Campbell's Act) provided for the first time that truth could be a defense provided it was also established that it was for the public benefit that the truth should be written. (Faulks Committee, p. 120.)

Prior to that time, truth had been no defense. Because the gravamen of the crime was the potential incitement to breach of the peace rather than protection of reputation, it was said that the "greater the truth the greater the libel," a line created, perhaps, by Lord Mansfield, and popularized by Robbie Burns in "The Reproof":

> "Dost know that old Mansfield
> Who writes like the Bible,
> Says the more 'tis a truth, sir,
> The more 'tis a libel?"

The Newspaper Libel and Registration Act of 1881 provided that if a newspaper were charged with criminal libel, a magistrate could go into the case, and, if he thought a jury would be likely to acquit, he could dismiss it.

Notwithstanding the decline in the use of the common law crime of libel in England as a tool against seditious libel, it was nevertheless used not infrequently in cases of defamatory libel. For example, between 1950 and 1973, there were an average of two such prosecutions per year, and many more complaints were considered by the police in each of those years (*Ibid.*, pp. 120-121.)

The common law crime of criminal libel was firmly inbedded in American jurisprudence by the time of the American Revolution. In the famous trial of Peter Zenger for criminal libel in 1735, his lawyer, Andrew Hamilton, did not challenge the legitimacy of the offense or its application to a prosecution for criticism of a public official. The prosecution was based upon the publication in the "New York Weekly Journal" of criticism of the action of the Royal Governor, William Cosby, for his dismissal of Chief Justice Lewis Morris. Although the jury's only technical function was to decide whether or not Zenger had published the article and truth was not, in any event, a defense, Hamilton persuaded them that they should acquit by arguing that truth could not be libelous.

Criminal libel became a public issue in the early days of the United States as a result of the passage in 1798 of the Sedition Act by the new federal government. That statute made it a crime subject to a fine of $2000 and two years years in prison to publish false, scandalous, and malicious material regarding the government of the United States, Congress, or the President with intent to defame or to bring them into contempt or disrepute. Unlike the common law crime, truth was to be a defense and the jury was to be the judge of both law and facts.

This provoked extensive contemporaneous debate over the significance of the First Amendment in relation to criticism of government and the new philosophy underlying the government of the United States. A corollary of the compact theory of government was that if the powers of the government were derived from the people, then the latter rather than the former should retain the power of criticism. James Madison summed it up in these words:

> "If we advert to the nature of Republican Government, we shall find that the censorial power is in the people over the Government, and not in the Government over the people." (4 Annals of Cong., p. 934 [1794].)

Although there were prosecutions under the act, its validity was never judicially examined by the Supreme Court, and it expired by its terms in 1801. Early in the nineteenth century, on the assumption that the act had been unconstitutional, Congress passed legislation authorizing repayment of fines levied under the Act.

Although this seemed to put an end to criminal libel at the federal level, that was by no means true of the states. In 1952, for example, according to Justice Frankfurter, writing in *Beauharnais v. People*:

"Today, every American jurisdiction—the forty-eight states, the District of Columbia, Alaska, Hawaii, and Puerto Rico—punish libels directed at individuals." (343 U.S. 250, 255, 72 S.Ct. 725, 729-30 [1952].)

Subject to Supreme Court limitations on the application of criminal libel to criticism of public officials, criminal libel is technically alive at the state level in the United States to this day, although prosecutions have apparently declined in number almost to the vanishing point.

The Supreme Court began its excursion into state regulation of public speech in 1925. In that year the Court for the first time announced that among the Fourteenth Amendment liberties protected from impairment by the states were rights under the First Amendment. *Gitlow v. New York* (268 U.S. 652, 45 S.Ct. 625 [1925]) was an appeal from a conviction under a New York statute outlawing criminal anarchy, that is, advocacy of the overthrow of the government by force or violence or by the assassination of the executive head of the government. The Supreme Court upheld the statute, announcing as the test whether the words are used in such circumstances and are of such a nature as to create a clear and present danger that they will bring about the substantive evils which the state has the right to prevent. Then in *Near v. Minnesota* (283 U.S. 697, 51 S.Ct. 625 [1931]), the Supreme Court, while laying down the principle that there can be no prior restraint on public speech, specifically stated that the federal Constitution does not prohibit prosecution of criminal libels by the states.

Later, in 1952 the Supreme Court in *Beauharnais*

v. People (343 U.S. 250, 72 S.Ct. 725 [1952]) upheld an Illinois criminal libel statute making it a crime to publish material portraying depravity, criminality, unchastity, or lack of virtue in any class of citizens of any race, color, creed, or religion when such material exposes the class to obloquy, contempt, or derision or when it promotes breach of the peace or riots. The defendant was prosecuted and convicted based on the circulation of leaflets portraying blacks as immoral and calling on the mayor to prevent further encroachment by blacks in white neighborhoods. By a narrow margin of 5-to-4, the Court reasoned that since such comments directed to an individual would justify a prosecution for libel, the same aimed at a group should stand on the same footing. The dissenters condemned the majority for not recognizing a constitutionally protected right to petition the government for redress of grievances.

Then, in a case styled *Garrison v. Louisiana* (379 U.S. 64, 85 S.Ct. 209 [1964]), the companion of *New York Times v. Sullivan*, the centerpiece of the final portion of this paper, the Supreme Court upset the conviction of a Louisiana district attorney for severely criticizing eight judges for their alleged lack of diligence in pursuing their duties. He was prosecuted under a Louisiana statute which made it a crime to publish maliciously anything exposing a person to hatred, contempt, or ridicule. Under the statute, if the published material was false, it was presumed to be malicious; if it was true, malice had to be proved.

Justice Brennan, speaking for the Court, stated that the qualification on the defense of truth in the statute, namely that it not only must be true but that it be

published "without malice," meaning publication
with good motives and for justifiable ends, could not
stand where the publication concerns public officials
and the conduct of their public business. In such
circumstances, truth must be an absolute defense.
Furthermore, even if the publication is false, a
different standard must apply. It is not enough that
malice in the sense of intent to inflict harm be proved.
Rather, First Amendment malice is required, that is,
either knowing falsehood or publication with reckless
disregard for whether it was true or false. Where the
matter does not concern the official conduct of a
public official, the former standard may still be
appropriate.

One further limitation on criminal libel was imposed by the Supreme Court. In 1966 in *Ashton v.
Kentucky* (384 U.S. 195, 86 S.Ct. 1407 [1966]) the
Court was faced with an appeal from a conviction for
the common law crime of libel. During a bitter coal
miners' strike, a leaflet was circulated stating, among
other things, that the Sheriff had engaged in acts of
brutality toward the strikers. The trial court defined
the crime with which the defendants were charged in
the absence of a statute as any false writing calculated
to create disturbances of the peace. The Kentucky
appellate court redefined the crime as simply the
publication of defamatory statements about another
which are false and made with malice. This redefini-
tion took place because *Near v. Minnesota* had eliminated the historic predicate of criminal libel, potential
breach of the peace, as a constitutionally acceptable
basis for imposing criminal liability. It then upheld
the conviction.

The Supreme Court reversed the lower court, holding that since the English common law crime of libel is inconsistent with constitutional restrictions and since no Kentucky case had redefined the crime in understandable terms, the elements of the crime were so indefinite that it could not be constitutionally enforced.

Thus, broadly speaking, in both the states of the United States and in England, libel may still be prosecuted as a crime. Although the original primary state interest being protected, the prevention of breach of the peace, may for constitutional reasons no longer be part of the rationale in the United States, the Supreme Court has clearly left open the possibility of state criminal prosecution for libel under a properly articulated criminal standard. And, if *Garrison v. Louisiana* still has vitality, which it may not, such a statute could be applied to the libel of a public official provided it incorporates the First Amendment malice standard.

The Sullivan Era

With *New York Times v. Sullivan* the libel laws of England and the United States began to diverge sharply with respect to their treatment of public officials and what have come to be called public figures. Beginning with that case, the Supreme Court embraced as a principle the need to provide "breathing space" for the erroneous statements which are perceived as inevitable in free debate if the "freedoms of expression" are to survive. Using the First Amendment as the implement and the need to

insure "that debate on public issues should be uninhibited, robust and wide open" as the battle cry, the
Court proceeded to eviscerate the long-established
state remedies for defamation. There is no English
counterpart to this development in the United States.

In March 1960, an advertisement appeared in the
New York Times which contained incorrect characterizations of police response to black civil rights demonstrations in Montgomery, Alabama. The police
commissioner of that city, L. B. Sullivan, brought a
libel suit against the paper, claiming that those incorrect characterizations defamed him. Sullivan
offered no evidence of pecuniary loss, but a jury
awarded him $500,000 and the Alabama Supreme
Court affirmed the award. The New York Times
Company appealed, and the Supreme Court reversed. It held the Alabama law under which Sullivan
recovered to be unconstitutional. Under that law,
general damages were presumed and punitive damages were available once libel per se was proven.
Although truth was a defense, good motives or mere
belief in the truth of the published statements were
relevant only to mitigation of punitive damages in the
jury's discretion.

The Supreme Court created a new standard. It held
that a public official cannot recover damages for a
defamatory falsehood regarding his official conduct
unless he proves that the statement was made either
with what the Court called "actual malice," which it
defined as knowledge that the statement was false, or
with reckless disregard of whether it was false or not.
(376 U.S. 252, 279-280, 84 S.Ct. 710, 726.)

Two years later in *Curtis Publishing Company v.*

Butts (388 U.S. 130, 87 S.Ct. 1975 [1967]), a plurality of the court extended the actual malice rule to so-called "public figures" in addition to public officials. Butts was a well-known college football coach who had successfully claimed damages from a magazine publishing company for an article which defamed him. The judgment in his favor was affirmed.

In 1968, in *St. Amant v. Thompson* the Supreme Court defined what it meant by "reckless disregard," the second prong of the actual malice test. St. Amant, a candidate for public office in Louisiana, defamed a deputy sheriff on a television program. The deputy sheriff sued and recovered $5,000. The finding of actual malice was based on evidence that St. Amant had no knowledge of the deputy sheriff's activities and made no attempt to verify his accusations before repeating what he had heard from a third party. The Supreme Court said this was not enough to establish reckless disregard, that it is not measured by whether a reasonably prudent publisher would have gone forward or would have investigated further. Instead, reckless disregard required a showing that the defendant "entertained serious doubts as to the truth of his publication." (390 U.S. 727, 731, 88 S.Ct. 1323, 1325 [1968].)

The high-water mark of the extension of the actual malice standard was reached in *Rosenbloom v. Metromedia, Inc.* (403 U.S. 29, 91 S.Ct. 1811 [1971].) There a radio broadcast contained defamatory comments regarding an individual who distributed adult magazines. It accused him of selling obscene materials. The individual was totally unknown to the public. A badly divided Supreme Court went beyond the public official, public figure tests and created a "public interest" exception to the general rule. Because the publication concerned obscenity laws, a matter of public interest, the Court said the actual malice standard should apply.

The Supreme Court promptly backed away from this public interest test three years later in *Gertz v. Robert Welch, Inc.* In that case, a magazine article was published following the conviction of a police officer for the murder of a black youth. The article accused Gertz, a lawyer who had been retained by the murdered youth's family to represent it in a civil action against the police officer, of misconduct. The alleged misconduct consisted of masterminding a frame-up, of having a criminal record, and of having been an official of a communist organization. Gertz sued, and although he offered no proof of special damages, the jury awarded him $50,000. The district court granted judgment notwithstanding the verdict on the basis of *New York Times.*

When *Gertz* reached the Supreme Court, an again-divided Court overruled *Rosenbloom*, deciding that the state's interest in protecting the private individual against defamation outweighs the countervailing First Amendment rights of the press. The court reasoned that private individuals have less access to the media than do public officials or public figures and have not thrust themselves into the public eye. The "events of public interest" test was inadequate to safeguard the state's interest in safeguarding individuals from injury to reputation. As a result, the Court concluded that "so long as they do not impose liability without fault, the States may define for themselves the appropriate standard of liability for a publisher or broadcaster of defamatory falsehood injurious to a private individual." Nonetheless, the Court said, because the states lack a substantial interest in awarding gratuitous money damages in excess of actual injury, they cannot allow presumed or punitive damages unless based on actual malice. (418 U.S. 323, 347, 349, 94 S.Ct. 2997, 3010, 3012 [1974].)

Then, in another shift, the Supreme Court seemingly backtracked on one aspect of *Gertz*. In 1985, in *Dun and Bradstreet, Inc. v. Greenmoss Builders, Inc.* (105 S.Ct. 2939 [1985]), the Court held that the *Gertz* prohibition on the award of presumed and punitive damages without a showing of actual malice did not apply to actions against nonmedia defendants when a matter of public concern is not involved. Because of the reduced value of speech regarding matters of purely private concern, the Court said that the state interest in compensating private individuals for injury to reputation is sufficient to support presumed or punitive damages without a showing of actual malice.

Thus, today, in the United States, the First Amendment guarantee of free speech precludes civil recovery for defamatory falsehood in suits by public officials or public figures unless actual malice is proved. There is now an open question, however, as to whether the malice rule applies where, in the case of a public official, the defamation concerns a matter unrelated to his public duties or function or, in the case of a public figure, to matters not germane to the controversy which is the basis of his public-figure status. Furthermore, in an action by a private individual against a media defendant, while states may permit recovery of actual damages, they may not award either presumed or punitive damages absent actual malice. However, in suits initiated by private plaintiffs against private defendants involving matters of private concern, the actual malice standard finally disappears.

Most recently, the Supreme Court in *Philadelphia Newspapers, Inc. v. Hepps* (106 S.Ct. 1558 [1986]) dealt with a newspaper story asserting that a franchisor of small stores selling beer, soft drinks, and snacks had links to organized crime. The trial court's charge imposed the burden of proof as to falsity on the plaintiff, and the jury returned a verdict for the defendant.

The Supreme Court affirmed a holding that at least in a case where a private individual was suing a media defendant for speech of public concern, the common law rule imposing the burden of proof as to truth on the defendant could not apply. It specifically reserved decision on the applicability of this rule to the case of the private individual suing the nonmedia defendant. (106 S.Ct. 1558, 1564, 1565, n. 4.)

These cases have substantially changed the law of defamation in the United States, and, for the first time since Independence, produced significant differences between the defamation law of this country and that of England.

There is first and obviously the change in the presumption of falsehood. In England the traditional rule is followed: Once proof of publication of defamatory matter is given, a cause of action has been made out, and truth is a matter for the defense with the burden of proof upon the defendant. In the United

States, at least where public officials or public figures are plaintiffs and the matter relates either to the conduct of a public office or a matter germane to the public controversy which is the basis of the public figure status, there is no presumption of falsehood; rather the plaintiff must prove not only publication of defamatory matter but also that it was false and that the defendant published with knowledge that it was false or with reckless disregard for whether it was true or not, reckless disregard meaning not some form of gross negligence, but serious doubts as to the truth of what was being published.

On the other hand, where the matter involves a suit by private plaintiffs suing private nonmedia defendants regarding matters of private concern, the states may still be free to indulge the presumption of falsehood and, subject to the reservation in *Hepps*, impose the burden of proof as to truth upon the defendant.

In the *Gertz* situation—that is, where a private figure is suing a media defendant over a matter of public concern—it would appear that the plaintiff would have the burden of proof on the issue of falsity but would not have to prove First Amendment malice to make out a cause of action and recover damages for "actual injury."

In England, the common law rule does not require proof of fault. Proof of innocent publication of defamatory matter is sufficient to make out a cause of action. In other words, a rule of strict liability is applied. In the United States, the *Sullivan* malice rule automatically subsumes strict liability in the cases to which it applies. In addition, the Court in *Gertz* held that the states could define the appropriate standard of liability for the publisher of defamatory falsehoods about a private individual only so long as they did not impose liability without fault. (418 U.S. 323, 347, 94 S.Ct. 2997, 3010 [1974].) Thus some proof of negligence is required in all cases.

It is not clear whether *Greenmoss* represents a retreat from this aspect of *Gertz* as well. The Court opinion in *Greenmoss* does not specifically address this issue, and it does allude in passing to the failure of the defendant to follow its usual practice of re-checking data regarding bankruptcies before it is published, which might be taken as evidence of negligence. The precise holding dealt only with presumed and punitive damages, i.e., that "permitting recovery of presumed and punitive damages in defamation cases absent a showing of 'actual malice' does not violate the First Amendment when the defamatory statements do not involve matters of public concern." Justice White in his concurring opinion interprets the Court's opinion (by three justices) as abrogating the *Gertz* requirement of proof of negligence as well (105 S.Ct. 2939, 2953), and that of Justice Burger reaches the same result. (*Id.*, at 2948.) If Justice White is correct, then the states, in cases to which neither *Sullivan* nor *Gertz* apply, are free to apply a strict liability standard without proof of negligence; in other words, the common law rule.

As is implicit in the above recital of changes, a difference in the law of damages is created. In England the common law rule still applies as to general damages. "General damages" are presumed from proof of publication of defamatory information, and a plaintiff is always entitled to nominal damages.

Presumed damages are intended to compensate for injury to reputation and to the plaintiff's feelings. Social disadvantages as well as natural grief and distress are taken into account. If there has been high-handed, oppressive, or contumelious behavior by the defendant which increases mental pain and suffering, general damages may be increased to take account of these aggravating factors. Special damages are also recoverable if proved, covering actual pecuniary loss suffered. Exemplary or punitive damages are recoverable only in the limited circumstance where the defendant has calculated that the money he will make by publishing the defamation exceeds the damages he will have to pay. (28 *Halsbury's Laws of England* 10 [4th ed. 1979].)

In the United States, the law of damages is slightly more complicated. In any case in which a plaintiff (whether a public official, public figure, or private figure) sustains the burden of proof as to First Amendment malice, the full range of common law damages (normal, presumed, special, and punitive) will be available.

In the *Gertz*-type case—that is, a private figure suing a media defendant over a matter of public concern—unless there is proof of First Amendment malice, recovery will be limited to compensation for "actual injury." This, the Court said, was not confined to actual out-of-pocket loss and need not be pecuniary in nature. It includes compensation for impairment of reputation and standing in the community, personal humiliation, mental anguish, and suffering, provided such damages are supported by competent proof. They cannot be presumed.

Finally, in the case of the private plaintiff suing a private defendant over a matter not of public interest, the full range of common law damages will be available without proof of First Amendment malice.

The Supreme Court in these cases also widened an already significant divergence in the qualified privilege of "fair comment" as it is applied in England and the United States. In England fair comment as formulated at common law is a defense to a claim of defamation. Fair comment is defined as "an expression of opinion on any matter of public interest." It is intended to protect expression of opinion (as distinct from statements of fact) where such opinion is actually defamatory. As with all qualified privileges, it is lost if abused. It is abused if it is published with common law malice or for any indirect or improper motive. (Faulks Committee, pp. 38-46.)

By the Defamation Act of 1952, a significant exception was carved out. Section 10 of that act provided that defamatory statements published by or on behalf of any candidate for Parliament or local government office should not be deemed privileged. (19 *Halsbury's Statutes of England* 34, 41 [3d ed.].) In the United States, on the other hand, the movement has been in the opposite direction. By virtue of *dicta* in *Gertz* expressions of opinion in public communications on matters of public concern, at least, are to be absolutely privileged. (418 U.S. 323, 339-40, 44 S.Ct. 2997, 3007.) Thus public criticism in the form of expression of opinion regarding public officials or public figures would not be actionable under any circumstances.

Gertz, moreover, has stimulated judicial interest in

the "opinion" escape valve for defendants in defamation cases and promoted the creation of new confusion as to the difference between fact and opinion and the expansion of the latter. A 1984 D.C. Circuit Court of Appeals case dealt with statements in a newspaper column that a college professor was, among other things, a "Marxist," and that his avowed purpose was to use the classroom to make revolutionaries. In affirming a grant of summary judgment for the defendants on the ground that the statements were constitutionally protected opinion, the court, en banc, produced no less than seven different opinions running to sixty-nine pages expressing differing views as to how under *Gertz* opinion and fact are now to be distinguished. (*Ollman v. Evans,* 750 F.2d 970 [D.C. Cir. 1984].) Furthermore, those publishing defamatory factual material regarding public officials or public figures (which would include candidates for public office) will not be liable unless there is proof of publication with First Amendment malice, a higher standard than common law malice.

In addition to the foregoing significant differences in the law of defamation, which are the product of *Sullivan* and its progeny, there are other differences which impact defamation litigation in significant ways.

A most important one is discovery. In the United States, under the Federal Rules of Civil Procedure, there is practically no limit to possible document discovery, deposition discovery, and discovery by interrogatory. Under Rule 26(b)(1), discovery may be had regarding any material which is relevant to the subject matter involved in the pending actions, and it is no objection that it would be inadmissible at trial if the information sought appears reasonably calculated to lead to the discovery of admissible evidence. Permitted discovery is so broad that these rules have led to considerable abuse and to frequent revision in an attempt to bring discovery under control. Where the parties are so inclined these discovery rules can be used to cause an enormous increase in the cost of litigation. (Fed. R. Civ., P. 26(b) advisory committee's note.)

Following *Sullivan* and the establishment of the First Amendment malice standard, the Supreme Court in *Herbert v. Lando* held that discovery could be had as to the editorial processes leading to the publication of the article. (441 U.S. 153, 99 S.Ct. 1635 [1979].) Thus, drafts of the offending article, memos written abut it, reporters' notes, and deposition testimony regarding the manner in which the article was reviewed internally before publication are all subject to discovery.

Under English law, on the other hand, discovery is severely limited. It occurs only after the pleadings have been closed, that is, after the issues have been reduced to final form. At that point, each party furnishes a list of the documents, if any, relating to the matters in issue which he has or has had in his possession. The other party has the right to inspect these documents. Normally discovery as to manuscripts is not permitted, but under a special statute it is possible to secure the discovery of the names of the printer, publisher, or proprietor of any newspaper or of any matters relative to the printing or publishing of any newspaper. (P. Carter-Ruck and R. Walker, *Carter-Ruck on Libel and Slander*, pp. 94-96 [3d ed.

1985]; 28 *Halsbury's Laws of England*, pp. 102-106 [4th ed. 1979].)

Thus an English plaintiff or defendant cannot rely upon notice pleading and unlimited discovery to ascertain the facts which will enable him to frame specific factual issues. He must be able to particularize those in his pleadings before he is entitled to discovery and that discovery is limited.

In this connection, one other aspect of English discovery practice is particularly noteworthy. Courts in a defamation action against a newspaper or other periodical will not require disclosure of the name of the person who supplied the information on which the alleged libel is based. The reason is, in part, that this information is not relevant to the plaintiff's case, since truth and the publisher's state of mind are not part of his *prima facie* case, and, in part, that its tendency to dry up a newspaper's sources of information would be against public policy. The rule was recently codified by the Contempt of Court Act of 1981. (Carter-Ruck, pp. 95-96.)

Another important difference concerns the matter of legal fees. Under English practice, legal fees are included in the costs borne by the losing party. Thus an unsuccessful plaintiff in a defamation action must bear not only his own but also the defendant's costs of counsel. (37 *Halsbury's Laws of England*, 547 [4th ed. 1979].) Under the law of the United States, counsel fees are not as a general rule part of the "costs" which may be awarded to the winning party. Evidence of such costs, however, has sometimes been admitted as relevant to the issue of punitive damages in defamation cases.

English Consideration of *Sullivan*

It is noteworthy that there has been formal consideration of the *Sullivan* revolution in England. In 1971, a Committee on Defamation was appointed by the British government. The Committee was chaired by the Honorable Mr. Justice Faulks and included judges, a university chancellor, a headmistress, journalists, authors, and barristers. It was charged with considering whether in the light of the working of the Defamation Act of 1952 "any changes are desirable in the law, practice and procedure relating to actions for defamation." It made its report in March 1975, having solicited views and testimony from every segment of British society and re-examined almost every aspect of the law of defamation.

One of the matters it considered was the desirability of adopting the *Sullivan* rule in the United Kingdom. It was assisted in this endeavor by a comprehensive summary of United States case law prepared by Harold R. Medina, Jr., counsel for *Time-Life* and *Fortune*, and by his live testimony in explication.

The Committee observed that one of the bases of *Sullivan*, i.e., the First Amendment, was a result of a premise of the Constitution of the United States, not applicable in the United Kingdom. As articulated by James Madison in a Report to the General Assembly of Virginia in 1798, that premise was that "The people, not the Government, possess the absolute sovereignty. . . . This form of government was altogether different from the British form under which the Crown was sovereign and the people were subjects." (Faulks Committee, p. 168.)

It also pointed out that the First and Fourteenth Amendments to the United States Constitution have no counterpart in England.

Of the rule advocated by Justice Black in *Rosenbloom v. Metromedia, Inc.*, the Committee concluded that such a "carte blanche to the press would be intolerable." (*Ibid.*) That rule, of course, was that with respect to matters of public or general concern, the media should be immune to libel judgments, even when publication was made with knowledge that it was false.

The Committee also noted that the simple negligence standard advocated by Justices Marshall and Harlan dissenting in *Rosenbloom v. Metromedia, Inc.* was akin to a reform proposal in England which had been debated in the House of Lords and not adopted.(*Id.*, p. 169.) That proposal would have made it a defense that the publisher of a false defamatory statement had taken all reasonable steps to ascertain the truth of the matter.

The Committee then concluded: "No English witness who gave evidence before us advocated the adoption of this new American principle in this country. We oppose it most strongly because we believe that here it would in many cases deny a just remedy to defamed persons." (*Ibid.*) Among those witnesses were representatives of every substantial media organization or member in the United Kingdom. (*Id.*, pp. 225-230.)

One British lawyer active in the defamation field, Mr. Geoffrey Robertson, Q.C., commented at the ABA Conference celebrating the twentieth anniversary of the *Sullivan* case that the reason no English witness advocated acceptance of *New York Times v. Sullivan* was that they were concentrating on a fallback position, the reasonable care proposal mentioned above, which was also rejected by the Faulks Committee. He also noted in passing that, as of 1984, no English case had even cited *Sullivan*.

Another member of the English legal profession has stated that the political climate there was different and much less deferential to the media as an institution than in the United States. One result of this is hesitancy on the part of the media to open too wide the libel reform door for fear the result would be less rather than more protection for the press. As indicative of the general climate, the comment was made that if Labour were to win the next election, a mandatory Press Council system for providing defamation redress was likely to be enacted to broaden the limited access to relief now represented by the expense of bringing an action in the High Court.

The Faulks Committee recommended a number of modifications in English libel law. These included several aimed at controlling damages. It was recommended that punitive damages be eliminated, that juries be partially eliminated (with judges in all cases determining the amount of damages), and that appellate courts be given the power to modify damage awards without the need for remand and a new trial. At the same time, it made a recommendation intended to mitigate the unfairness of the cost barrier to defamation actions by extending Legal Aid under the Legal Aid Act of 1974 to defamation actions, the only cause of action then excluded. (Faulks Committee, pp. 172-188.) None of these recommended changes has been adopted.

Media Dissatisfaction in the United States

Notwithstanding the substantial additional protections the media now enjoy in the United States as compared with its English counterparts, there is widespread dissatisfaction here among the media with the present state of the law of defamation.

The concerns expressed center around three points. One is the size of verdicts in defamation cases. Another is the tremendous cost of litigation both in terms of out-of-pocket expense and management and editorial time. The third is that the First Amendment malice standard puts in issue the state of mind of the publisher at the time of publication. This results, according to the Supreme Court's *Herbert v. Lando* decision, in permitted discovery of every detail of the editorial process by which the offending material was brought into being. The impact of these characteristics is said to have a substantial "chilling" effect upon the media's ability and willingness to perform their constitutional function, that it will result and has resulted in self-censorship.

There have certainly been a number of eye-catching libel verdicts in the United States in the 1980s. Among these are a $40,300,000 verdict in *Guccione v. Hustler Magazine, Inc.*, $40,000,000 in *Lerman v. Flynt*, $26,000,000 in *Pring* (Miss Wyoming) *v. Penthouse*, $9,200,000 in *Green v. Alton Telegraph Printing Co.*, $4,500,000 in the 1981 trial in *McCoy v. Hearst Corp.*, $5,050,000 in *Brown and Williamson Tobacco Corp. v. Jacobson*, $2,900,000 in *Thompson v. Combined Communications of Kentucky*, $2,050,000 in *Tavoulareas v. Washington Post*, $1,600,000 in *Carol Burnett v. National Enquirer*, and $1,250,000 in *Macnieder v. Diaz*. (Sack and Tofel, *First Steps Down the Road Not Taken: Emerging Limitations on Libel Damages*, 90 Dick. L. Rev. 609, 610-11 nn. 11, 14 & 16-17 [1986].)

According to the Libel Defense Resource Center, a media-sponsored source of statistics on the subject, while only one pre-1980 libel award exceeded $1,000,000, fully 60 percent of the 1983 jury awards surpassed that figure. In the 1980-1983 period, excluding three eight-figure verdicts against *Penthouse* and *Hustler* magazines, the average libel award was $871,891. One commentator, citing figures, asserts that since 1982 million dollar plus verdicts in libel cases have become routine. (*Id.*, p. 611.)

Another 1984 Libel Defense Resource Center study has concluded that damage awards by juries in libel and privacy actions against the media exceed jury awards in medical malpractice and product liability cases. The study showed that damage awards in libel actions averaged more than $2,000,000 each, while jury awards in product liability cases in a comparable period averaged $785,651, and awards in medical malpractice cases averaged $665,764. The largest component of the awards was punitive damages with compensatory damages averaging slightly over $550,000, a figure well below the average for medical malpractice and product liability cases. (*Punitive Damages in Libel Actions*, Record of the Association of the Bar of the City of New York, Vol. 42, No. 1 Jan./Feb. 1987, 20, 39-40, 54 n. 102.)

In response, it is pointed out that these same Legal Defense Resource Center studies show that these large jury verdicts are the exception rather than the rule. In the first place, these studies indicated that the media successfully disposes of 75 percent of defamation cases on motion before trial, and, although plaintiffs win 90 percent of those which go to trial, a very high percentage of the large jury verdicts are either reduced or vacated by the appellate courts. (*Punitive Damages in Libel Actions*, p. 64; Association of the Bar of the City of New York, Vol. 42, No. 1 Jan./ Feb. 1987; Kaufman, *Libel 1980-1985: Promises and Realities*, 90 Dick. L. Rev. 545, 550 [1986].) The 90 percent figure covered the period 1980-1982 and was not significantly different from the 83 percent loss figure of 1976-1980. An LRDC study of the years 1982-1984 showed a sharp drop in that loss rate to 60 percent, but that figure compares unfavorably to other tort actions where defendants generally win 60 to 70 percent of the cases tried. (Kaufman, p. 552.)

According to a different commentator, of the libel cases brought, 75 percent are dismissed before trial; plaintiffs secure a jury verdict 85 percent of the time, but trial judges grant j.n.o.v. motions in 20 percent of these cases, and in the appeals from all other adverse verdicts the plaintiff loses his judgment two-thirds of the time. In all, plaintiffs who sue media defendants win and keep a judgment in only about 5 to 10 percent of all libel cases brought, and most, after all appeals, obtain relatively small dollar awards. (Franklin, *Good Names and Bad Law: A Critique of Libel Law and a Proposal*, 18 U.S.F. L. Rev. 1, 4-5 [1983].)

The 1984 L.R.D.C. study concluded that the danger posed by megaverdicts was greatly exaggerated and that the size of verdicts was actually declining. (Assn. of the Bar Dissent, pp. 64-65.) One of the most recent ot these L.R.D.C. studies focuses on libel actions brought by public officials. It concluded that the total number of judgments finally collected by public official plaintiffs was a tiny fraction of all actions commenced. Of greater importance, the average collected in that tiny fraction of cases over the period 1976 to 1984 was just under $85,000. (Assn. of the Bar Dissent, p. 72, n. 39.)

This latter study is of considerable significance to the debate over one reform proposal. That proposal, articulated in the concurring opinion in *Sullivan* by Justices Black, Douglas, and Goldberg, would accord absolute privilege to "criticism of the way public officials do their public duty." (376 U.S. 254, 293, 84 S.Ct. 710, 733.) That study would seem to indicate that the *Sullivan* rule was working reasonably well in regard to criticism of public officials, at least with respect to damages collected.

Concern has been expressed particularly regarding the size of punitive damages awards and, also, of the presumed damage component of general damages where it is left to the jury to put a value on the injury to the plaintiff's reputation, his wounded feelings, humiliation, and resulting physical pain or illness. Attention is directed to the *Guccione* case where $37,000,000 of a $40,300,000 award was punitive damages; similarly as to $33,000,000 of the $40,000,000 verdict in the *Lerman* case. (Sack and Tofel, p. 611, n. 14.) Attention is also directed to *McCoy v. Hearst Corp.* where two policemen and a prosecutor sued a newspaper over a report that the three had engaged in brutality and subornation of perjury in a murder case to secure a conviction. The only evidence of injury was the plaintiffs' testimony that they felt their careers had been damaged and the results would be with them for the rest of their lives. They also testified as to the shock and emotional effects of the article. On the basis of this testimony, a jury awarded each compensatory damages of $1,000,000 and punitive damages of $520,000. (*Id.*, pp. 613-614.)

These would appear to be exceptional cases. Various of the Legal Resource Defense Center studies show that half the punitive damages awards were $25,000 or less, and another study by Professor Marc Franklin of Stanford University indicated that only 25 percent of plaintiffs in libel actions seek punitive damages. (Assn. of the Bar Dissent, pp. 64-65.)

As to the second point of dissatisfaction, namely costs of litigation other than the cost of judgments, these, indeed, can be substantial. One commentator reports estimates of the legal cost of defending General Westmoreland's suit against CBS at as high as $8,000,000, and the cost of *Time's* defense of the Ariel Sharon suit at as high as $7,000,000. It also reports a congressman's estimate of $150,000 as the average cost of defending a libel action. (Sack and Tofel, p. 610.)

William P. Tavoulareas testified at the hearing on

punitive damages in his libel action against the
Washington Post that the counsel fees he and his son
incurred to that point were $1,800,000. (Lewis, *New
York Times v. Sullivan Reconsidered: Time to Return
to "The Central Meaning of the First Amendment,"* 83
Colum. L. Rev. 603, 613 [1983].)

One commentator suggests that as much as 80
percent of the cost of libel insurance is accounted for
by the costs of defending these cases. And there can
be no doubt that substantial time of management,
editors, and reporters will be required in order to
prepare and present the defense in these cases. (Sack
and Tofel, p. 610.)

The very high cost of litigation is not a condition
peculiar to the defamation field. It is a characteristic
of the whole spectrum of litigation in our society. The
high cost flows largely from "notice" pleading
coupled with the liberal rules of discovery and the
monumental costs of handling the mountain of
evidentiary material which that discovery produces.
Where the parties have the resources and the inclination, those rules permit the use of discovery to run up
the cost of litigation and harass the other party. What
is needed is overall reform of the discovery rules in
order to correct this flaw in our legal system, rather
than a skewing of the substantive rules in one particular field of law.

It should also be noted that to a large extent these
costs are within the control of the parties and particularly of the media defendants. Their reluctance to
acknowledge error and their determination to vindi-
cate their editorial integrity by mounting in signifi-

cant cases a "no stones unturned" defense is what runs up the cost of litigation.

As to the third of these sources of dissatisfaction, there are widespread assertions that the threat of libel suits is "chilling" the editorial process in the United States. It is said that self-censorship "occurs whenever a reporter or editor omits a word, a passage, or an entire story not for journalistic reasons but because of the possible legal implications." The present standards of press protection propagate selfcensorship it is said, for two reasons. The press cannot readily determine whether an individual is a public or a private figure, and a virtually unreviewable jury verdict determines whether the constitutional standard is met. (Del Russo, *Freedom of the Press and Defamation: Attacking the Bastion of New York Times Co. v. Sullivan*, 25 St. Louis U.L.J. 501, 519 [1981].)

Remedies proposed by those of this view would move in the direction of greater immunity for the media. These hark back to *Sullivan* itself and the positions taken by Justices Black and Douglas, who advocated giving "the press an absolute immunity for criticism of the way public officials do their public duty" and "[an] unconditional right to say whatever one pleases about public affairs. . . ." Justice Goldberg, also joined by Justice Douglas, advocated "[a]n unconditional privilege to criticize official conduct despite the harm which may flow from excesses and abuses." (376 U.S. 254, 295-298, 84 S.Ct. 710, 734-735.)

Some commentators, starting from the plurality opinion in *Rosenbloom v. Metromedia, Inc.*, advocate absolute immunity on a subject-matter-related rather than a status-related (public official or public figure) basis. This advocates absolute immunity for the press where the matter discussed is one of "public or general concern." One of the main reasons given for this recommendation is the difficulty and confusion which has attended the application of the *Gertz* public figure standard and the resulting unpredictability of the result to an editor contemplating a particular story. (Del Russo, p. 520.)

The American Civil Liberties Union carried this one step further. In 1982, its governing board adopted a resolution endorsing the following: Absolute privilege to be accorded to any statements about a public official on matters related to his office, about public figures on matters related to their public status, and about anyone on a matter of public concern. The consensus seemed to be that reputation as a moral value in our society was entitled to zero weight in such cases. (Surkin, p. 668.)

At the intellectual level the debate proceeds around this issue. The nature and extent of the First Amendment guarantee of freedom of the press versus the state interest in the protection of the reputation of individuals. This leads to learned dissertations such as those by Del Russo and Lewis on the history and purpose of the First Amendment, leading to the conclusion that it occupies a "perferred position" among our constitutional freedoms. This in turn produces equally learned articles like that by Surkin asserting that the right of an individual to his good reputation is a fundamental right of equal importance, because it is closely allied with the fundamental concept of the presumption of innocence, one of the primary elements of constitutional due process.

It also produces articles challenging the factual and intellectual basis of conclusions that greater immunity should be accorded the media. One commentator points out that there is not unanimity on the issue of self-censorship. Prestigious publishers and broadcasters assert that libel law has not deterred them from practices they think appropriate. One reporter, after interviewing a number of editors and journalists, reported that not one ever killed a news account he believed was true and important because of fear of a libel suit. That same commentator points out that the often-cited statement of Justice Brandeis about the desirability of more speech rather than repression was not made in the context of defamation actions but in the context of abstract political debate. The same comment was made concerning John Stuart Mill's remark that false statements may make valuable contributions to public debate because their collision with truth will produce a clearer perception of that truth. (Franklin, pp. 16, 24-25.)

The real issue is the point at which a balance must be struck between the needs of society for both a vigorous and unrestrained press, and legal norms which will accord adequate protection to individual reputation. Before *Sullivan*, the balancing point was where it had been located for over a century and a half. The individual was presumed to have a good reputation, and if the media defamed him, it did so at its peril unless it could prove truth. *Sullivan* moved the balance point for public figures in the media's direction. The presumption was reversed. The media

was presumed to be publishing the truth and the
defamed individual not only had the burden of proving falsity but had to prove deliberate lying as well.
The Supreme Court, starting with *Sullivan,* concluded that perhaps the media needs some breathing
room, some margin for honest error in dealing with
public officials, public figures, and matters of public
interest, but it does not need immunity for the
deliberate lie. The initial balancing point apparently
worked well for more than a century and a half in the
United States. It is still working well in England.

Unless one is prepared to abandon security of
reputation as a moral value in a free society, it would
seem hard to justify further movement of the balancing point in the media's direction on either theoretical
or practical grounds. Given the history of the law of
defamation and its status at the time of the adoption of
the First Amendment, it cannot rationally be asserted
that that amendment was intended by its authors to
immunize the media from liability for libel under
state law.

Nor does it seem persuasive to argue that such immunity is required to ensure the survival of the media
in healthy financial form. When one looks at the size
and resources of the leading media elements in this
country, it is not plausible to believe that libel suits
are going to drive them into insolvency. *The New York
Times, The Washington Post,* CBS, NBC, ABC, Time
Inc., Gannett Newspapers, and many, many more are
all substantial well-financed business enterprises.
NBC is now owned by General Electric Company,
with a net worth of $13,904,000,000 as of year end
1985; ABC, by Capital Cities Communications, Inc.,

with a net worth of $889,200,000. CBS Inc. has a net worth of $669,700,000; the *New York Times*, a net worth of $558,000,000; the *Washington Post*, a net worth of $349,000,000; Gannett Co., a net worth of $1,275,200,000; Tribune Co., a net worth of $908,500,000; Dow Jones and Co., a net worth of $600,200,000; Knight-Ridder, a net worth of $696,600,000; Time Inc., a net worth of $1,210,500,000. (*Value Line*, 1986, 1987.)

Moreover, CBS and Time Inc. respectively demonstrated in the *Westmoreland* and *Sharon* cases that they are prepared and able to spend any amount necessary not only to win their lawsuits but also to inhibit or blunt any criticism of their conduct, both in publishing the articles and in defending the lawsuits. *Reckless Disregard*, a book written by Renata Adler which is critical of the methods and tactics used by these two defendants, was finally published only after negotiating numerous roadblocks constructed by CBS and Time and enduring substantial intimidation and peripheral disparagement of its author. (West, "A Trial by Furor for Renata Adler," *Insight*, Jan. 12, 1987, pp. 60-61.)

There are undoubtedly many small media enterprises and some noteworthy examples of libel judgments financially crippling to those enterprises. Leaving aside the issue of whether those judgments were morally and ethically, as well as legally, justified, it seems ingenuous to argue that a rule of protection calibrated for the small town weekly newspaper is necessary to ensure the health and viability of a critical mass of media in the United States. When one considers the existence and financial health of the enterprises listed above, so long as those giants are around, it is hard to imagine an absence of debate on public issues which is uninhibited, robust, and wide open.

The media argue that, to an extent which is immeasurable but substantial, the present situation has a chilling effect on the media's willingness to deal with controversial subjects and to engage in investigative reporting. There is undoubtedly truth in this assertion. But there is no empirical basis for measuring the extent or the impact of this effect. The Supreme Court today clearly recognizes that there is a trade-off which security of reputation requires, concluding that "the danger of self-censorship . . . [is] a valid, but not the exclusive, concern in suits for defamation: 'The need to avoid self-censorship by the news media . . . is not the only societal value at issue . . . [or] this Court would have embraced long ago the view that publishers and broadcasters enjoy an unconditional . . . immunity from liability for defamation.'" (*Gertz v. Robert Welch, Inc.*, 418 U.S. 323, 341, 97 S.Ct. 2997, 3007 [1974].)

If one reflects on the events of the last fifteen years starting with Watergate and ending with the Iran-Contra episode, it's difficult to believe that investigative reporting in the United States is either dead or seriously inhibited.

The Supreme Court has unequivocally stated that the deliberate lie is not entitled to constitutional protection. It has characterized the lie as being at odds with the premise of democratic government, and as making no contribution to orderly social progress. It, therefore, has no redeeming social value and deserves no constitutional protection. (*Garrison v. Louisiana*, 379 U.S. 64, 75, 85 S.Ct. 209, 216 [1964].)

Therefore, the solution to today's problem does not seem to lie in the direction of greater immunity for the media.

Other reform initiatives point in the direction of attempting to accommodate both interests on a basis which will not cripple the media or unwisely intimidate them. Congressman Schumer offered a bill in the Ninety-Ninth Congress which would have created a federal declaratory judgment action of truth, eliminated punitive damages, and freely granted attorneys' fees. (Sack and Tofel, p. 609, n. 3.)

A similar proposal was made by Professor Marc Franklin of Stanford Law School for what he termed an action for restoration of reputation. This would be a remedy in which the only issue would be the truth or falsity of the publication in issue. The burden of proof would be on the plaintiff, and he would have to meet this burden under the "evidence of convincing clarity" standard, which, incidentally, does not now even apply on that issue under the *Sullivan* rule. In addition, a necessary predicate to the action would be a request to the publisher for a retraction, and, in the subsequent action, the plaintiff would be limited to proof given to the publisher at that time, meaning, presumably, that the plaintiff would never have access through discovery to evidence in the hands of the publisher bearing on the issue of truth. If successful, the only recovery would be legal costs from the date of the defamatory publication. The plaintiff could only pursue this remedy, moreover, if he made an irrevocable election to abandon the modified conventional remedy which Franklin also espouses. (Franklin, pp. 40-47).

Another attempt to deal with these issues was the special verdict technique used by Judge Sofaer in the *Sharon* case, which had an unusual aspect. Judge Sofaer not only instructed the jury to decide separately whether the article was defamatory, whether it was false, and whether it was published with First Amendment malice, but he directed the jury to return to the courtroom to announce each part of the verdict as it was reached. The jury first announced a finding that the article was defamatory, two days later that it was false, but a week later that it had not been published with malice. (Norris, *Winning the War Against Self-Censorship: Eliminating Special Verdicts in Defamation Actions*, 90 Dick. L. Rev. 683, 684 [1986].) Although he recovered no damages in the United States, Sharon did achieve substantive vindication. Surprisingly, this use of the special verdict has been criticized as circumventing the constitutional protection intended for the media in defamation actions because it may encourage individuals interested in vindication rather than damages to sue, thus prompting increased self-censorship by the media.

While this argument may have some logic, it certainly seems calculated to produce a result undesirable from a public policy viewpoint, namely, to render more difficult the establishment of the truth about the veracity of the media. It's one thing to argue that the media should be protected from inhibiting financial liability. It's quite another to argue that the law should also serve the purpose of preventing public disclosure of the media's mistakes.

Other reform proposals pointing in the same direction have focused on damages alone. The modifications in common law damage rules resulting from *Gertz* have already been discussed. Justice Harlan, dissenting in *Rosenbloom v. Metromedia, Inc.*, urged that punitive and presumed damages be closely scrutinized and carefully limited. (403 U.S. 29, 72-77, 91 S.Ct. 1811, 1833-1836 [1971].) Justice Marshall, dissenting in the same case, suggested their elimination. (*Id.* at 78-87.) More recently, Justice White went further and suggested abandoning all or part of the *Sullivan* standard of liability in exchange for limitation on damages to the point where they would not unduly threaten the press. (*Dun and Bradstreet, Inc. v. Greenmoss Builders Inc.*, 105 S.Ct. 2939, 2948 [1985].)

Several commentators have called for the elimination of punitive damages and the exercise of greater control by the courts over excessive awards.

A synthesis of these reform ideas could provide a solution to today's defamation dilemma which would be more satisfactory to all concerned, and preserve the profound moral values in both security of reputation and freedom of expression.

Current English Experiences

It is relevant to the modest proposal with which this paper will conclude to digress and consider current British experience under their modern version of the old common law rules of defamation. Why is their experience different from that of the media in the United States? How have they managed to survive, prosper, and perform their Fourth Estate function without benefit of *Sullivan* and without constant agitation for some form of immunity?

The answers seem to lie first in a perception that security of reputation has a moral value in society at least equal to that of the need for a free press. It also is the result of a perception seldom mentioned in the United States, i.e., the possibility that a *Sullivan* rule would "chill" the willingness of able persons to enter public service for fear of false and damaging statements from those who have no regard for reputation.

A major reason the British media seem able to survive and prosper is a difference in the cost of defamation litigation. These costs are materially lower for three reasons. Jury verdicts are very much lower. Costs of litigation, including legal fees, appear to be lower even though costs which the loser bears will include the winner's legal fees. The third reason is that the media in England seem much more willing to settle libel claims than is the case in the United States.

An important difference is the size of jury awards in libel actions. According to one authoritative tabulation, from 1959 to early 1985 only five libel awards reached six figure amounts. Two of these arose out of the same incident and occurred in 1961, one for £100,000 and one for £117,000. A third occurred in Scotland in 1978 for £302,000. A fourth occurred in February 1982 for £100,000. The last was in 1984 for £253,000. Only two of these verdicts (1978 and 1982) were permitted to stand on appeal. Other awards in the 1976-1985 period ranged from one half-penny to £70,000, with an average (excluding the five larger awards mentioned above) of £18,479. In only two cases in this period were exemplary or punitive damages awarded, one in 1982 amounting to £15,000 of a £22,000 total award and the other £250,000 of a £253,000 total award in 1984. This latter award was set aside on appeal, and the case was subsequently settled for a small fraction of the original award. (Carter-Ruck, App. III.)

It should be noted that, according to the *New York Times*, a new record was set on July 24, 1987, when Jeffrey Archer, the bestselling novelist and former deputy chairman of the Conservative Party, was awarded £800,000 in damages in a libel action against a London tabloid. The defendant has said it would appeal. (*N.Y. Times*, July 25, 1987, p. 5, col. 5.)

It is interesting that in England, although juries have been abolished in most civil cases, and notwithstanding the Faulks Committee recommendation, they have been retained in libel actions. This appears to be because of the belief that such actions put in issue two matters peculiarly related to ordinary community standards, namely the ordinary meaning of words to ordinary people and the judgmental perception of human behavior on the basis of general current standards of opinion. On both of these issues, juries are thought to be better qualified than judges. This practice also seems to be based on the belief that juries are at least as capable as judges of fairly assessing damages, with the present system providing courts with the power to intervene in the exceptional case where the jury goes astray. (Faulks Committee, p. 124-146, 207-224 [Minority Report on Trial by Jury in Defamation Actions].)

Criticism of the jury role in these actions in England is echoed in the United States but with the added argument that juries are incapable of under-standing the complicated *Sullivan* rules. (Kaufman, "The Media and Juries," *N.Y. Times*, Nov. 4, 1982; Kaufman, pp. 545, 555.)

The situation as to costs of litigation is more difficult to measure precisely. A recent article in the *U.K. Press Gazette* states that lead counsel in a libel action will ask £7,500 to appear and expect "refreshers" of £750 to £1,000 per day after day one. The "silk" will expect to be accompanied by a junior barrister who will expect a fee of £4,000 to appear and refreshers of £350 to £500 per day. The solicitors will require at least £15,000 to bring the case to trial and will also ex-pect refreshers at a rate of about £750 per day. (Brett, "Defamation: Putting the Whole System on Trial," *U.K. Press Gazette*, Mar. 2, 1987, p. 20.)

Although these figures are undoubtedly modest compared with the cost of keeping a Cravath team in court and in the back room in a *Westmoreland* case, it should be remembered that the losing party bears not only his own costs but those of the winner as well. This same article suggests that in some cases total costs have been substantial. Reference is made to a BBC case in which the broadcaster paid an estimated £1,000,000 in legal costs, and to a second case in which it had to pay a plaintiff's legal costs of £250,000. (*Ibid.*) One solicitor for a British newspaper group estimates that a five-day libel trial would generate a total of £80,000 in legal fees for both sides.

When compared with estimates of defense costs alone of $8,000,000 in the *Westmoreland* case, and $7,000,000 in the *Sharon* case, the British figures seem modest, especially if one considers that the American figures cover only one side of the equation. They also seem modest compared with an estimate of $150,000 as the cost of defending the average libel case in the United States, meaning that the total cost may have been on the order of $300,000. (Sack and Tofel, p. 610.)

One major contributing factor to lower costs of litigation in England is their radically more limited rules of discovery. As already noted, in defamation actions, generally, no discovery is permitted until the pleadings are closed and the specific factual issues identified. Then discovery is limited to matter relating to those issues.

Two statutory enactments encourage and facilitate the early resolution of defamation disputes. One is the "amends" provision of Section 4 of the Defamation Act of 1952, which is intended to provide a defense for a publisher's unintentional defamation, that is, cases of statements not intended to refer to the plaintiff and cases of statements which are apparently innocuous, but, because of facts unknown to the publisher, are in fact defamatory. A prompt offer of "amends," that is, an offer to publish a suitable correction and a sufficient apology, to the party aggrieved and an offer to take reasonable steps to notify the parties to whom the offending words have been

distributed—all accompanied by an affidavit setting
forth the facts demonstrating the publisher's innocence—will constitute a defense to the action.
Although reported cases in which this defense has
been used are few, one commentator has stated that it
has in practice constituted an invaluable defense tool.
(Carter-Ruck, pp. 141-143.)

The other statutory enactment is the "payment into
court" provision of the Rules of the Supreme Court,
which apply generally to civil actions. A defendant
may, without the knowledge of the judge or jury,
notify the plaintiff of a payment into court in satisfaction of the plaintiff's claim. If the plaintiff elects not to
accept the payment and is awarded an amount greater
than the payment, he collects the judgment and his
costs. If his award is less than the payment, however,
he receives a judgment of only the amount of the
award and he must bear the defendant's costs including legal fees from the date of the payment on. One
other feature of the rule, applicable only in libel and
slander actions, encourages acceptance. The plaintiff
may, with the approval of the judge, be permitted to
make a statement in open court which would provide
him with the opportunity to restore his reputation. It
should be noted that the payment into court is not an
admission of liability, but only an offer to dispose of
the claim. Therefore, the plaintiff's statement will be
something short of a claim that the defendant has ex-
pressly admitted error. (*Id.*, pp. 150-152.) Such an
offer presents a plaintiff with a real dilemma because
of the great uncertainty of the amount of a jury's
verdict even when victory seems certain.

The payment into court practice is somewhat

similar to that covered by Rule 68 of Federal Rules of Civil Procedure in the United States. This authorizes an offer of judgment ten days before a trial begins with the consequence that if such is made but not accepted, and the judgment finally obtained is not more favorable, the offeree must bear costs incurred after the making of the offer. Those costs, of course, do not as a general rule in defamation actions include the legal fees of the opposing party, so that an offer of judgment under Rule 68 does not present a plaintiff with quite the dilemma his British counterpart faces.

Responses of a number of media lawyers in England to a request for comment on the state of British libel law and how the media manages under the rules of strict liability emphasize the role of settlement and provide a number of illuminating insights into the impact of all of these differences. They indicate a consensus on several points:

1. Cost is indeed the key element restraining libel litigation and, furthermore, fostering withdrawal, compromise, or settlement of 95 percent of the libel actions actually brought;

2. Investigative reporting is more restrained than in the United States, but it is also characterized by a higher degree of care, accuracy, and fairness;

3. Even representatives of the media do not believe that the adoption of the *Sullivan* rule would be desirable because of the belief that it would not only produce unfair results but would also do more public harm than good. (Private letters from Justin Walford, Group Assistant Legal

Adviser, Daily Express [May 8, 1987]; Henry R. Douglas, Legal Manager, News Group Newspapers, Ltd. [May 22, 1987]; H.R. Lat. Corrie, Director of Legal Services, Mirror Group Newspapers [May 13, 1987].)

One English barrister, speaking at an ABA Conference celebrating the twentieth anniversary of *New York Times v. Sullivan*, summed up the British view of *Sullivan* in these words:

"What then are the real objections of principle to the 'public figure' doctrine? We share, with American law, recognition of two competing interests: reputation restoration and free speech, but it seems to us that the 'public figure' doctrine abandons, in relation to one class of persons, the first interest almost entirely. It denies virtually any protection to persons who are prominent in public affairs, simply because of that fact. Persons in public life necessarily expose themselves to public criticism, accepting harsh comment and intrusion into home life which would be resented by a private citizen. There must come a point at which any public figure, however prominent, is entitled to some form of legal protection against the retailing of false and damaging statements. . . .

"This, I think, would be the authorised view from the mother country of the black sheep of the family, the pilgrim father who ran away to sea and became rich and famous by methods up with which we will not put . . ."(Remarks by Geoffrey Robertson, Q.C., ABA Conference celebrating

20th Anniversary of *New York Times v. Sullivan*, Washington, D.C. [1984].)

A Modest Proposal

Turning to the present unhappy plight of the black sheep, no solution to the current defamation dilemma of the United States will please everyone. It does seem, though, that a variation and synthesis of Justice White's suggestion in *Greenmoss* and Professor Franklin's proposal of a Restoration of Reputation action might go far toward alleviating both media and injured individual concerns.

Suppose the Supreme Court were to do the following:

1. In an appropriate defamation case on First Amendment grounds:

a. Overrule *Sullivan* and its progeny as not having served their intended purpose and reestablish the First Amendment legitimacy of the common law rule of strict liability;

b. Eliminate all presumed and punitive damages and restrict recovery to actual pecuniary loss, that is, to special damages redefined to include legal fees except where legal fees are included as taxable costs under state law, or, for cases pending in the Federal Courts, under Rule 54(d) of the Federal Rules of Civil Procedure.

2. In such case, either on First Amendment grounds or in the exercise of its general equitable powers (*Hall v. Cole*, 412 U.S. 1, 93 S.Ct. 1943 [1973]), specify that

costs recoverable under Rule 54(d) of the Federal
Rules of Civil Procedure will, in defamation cases, include legal fees.

3. In the exercise of its power under 28 U.S.C. 2072
to prescribe rules of procedure for the Federal District Courts:

a. Amend Rule 49(a) of the Federal Rules of Civil
Procedure relating to special verdicts to provide that
in all defamation cases special verdicts on the issues of
defamation, falsity, and damages will be required;

b. Amend Rule 68 of the Federal Rules of Civil
Procedure relating to offers of judgment to provide
that in defamation actions an offer solely of a money
judgment will qualify under the Rule, and in such
cases such offer may be made at any time prior to the
time when the defendant commences the presenta-
tion of his case.

This radical restructuring of defamation actions
would have a number of benefits. The state of mind of
the publisher and the editorial process by which the
article was written would no longer be issues in the
case. The chilling effect the existence of these issues
and discovery relating to them has had on the editorial process will no longer exist. The costs of discovery, trial preparation, and trial should be materially reduced by the elimination of those issues.

The effect of the elimination of these issues will,
moreover, be to refocus the action on the truth or
falsity of what has been printed or said. This is the
primary concern of a plaintiff, the public, and, presumably, the publisher. The requirement of special

verdicts as to that issue will also promote this focus of attention.

It would have one other substantial public policy benefit. Disclosure of sources would not automatically be an issue in every defamation case as it is now because the publisher's belief in the truth of what was published must be examined. Rather, it would only become a problem where a defendant had to rely on the oral testimony of a confidential source to establish a defense of truth, a matter within the control of the defendant.

The elimination of presumed and punitive damages would remove the danger of megaverdicts and their chilling effect on the media. It would also eliminate the danger perceived by some of the use by juries of large damage awards to punish unpopular ideas or people and those who appear to be advancing or protecting them.

The inclusion of legal fees in taxable costs has a number of substantial benefits. First, it enables a successful plaintiff to recover what is usually the biggest financial detriment he suffers as a result of a defamation incident, which is the cost of his lawyer. Second, it should tend to discourage the potential plaintiff and his lawyer who have a marginal case. A plaintiff whose lawyer is willing to proceed on a contingent fee basis has very little at risk. But if he faces the prospect of having to reimburse the defendant out of his own pocket for the latter's legal fees if he loses, he is likely to think twice before proceeding.

The suggested modification of Rule 68 relating to offers of judgment is intended to provide a media defendant with a substantial degree of control over even the comparatively modest financial exposure he would face under this modified system. It is also intended to provide him with an incentive to make a realistic appraisal of his case and to make an offer of settlement which would not have to include an explicit admission of error.

From the plaintiff's viewpoint, any such offer of judgment (which would automatically also import the offer of costs including legal fees to the date of the offer) would be difficult to decline. Acceptance would permit him to claim vindication and keep him whole as to his legal costs. His only gain from proceeding would be the possible explicit vindication of a jury verdict and the amount by which the sum offered fell short of his actual losses. Against these advantages would be the risk of having to bear both his own and the defendant's costs from that point on.

Finally, these reforms would return protection of reputation to its traditional place in society's pantheon of moral values, with minimum impairment of the media's ability to perform its function without fear of crippling losses. It should make libel insurance more reasonable in cost, and thus enable particularly the smaller media enterprise to follow more aggressive investigative reporting policies.

The return to the strict liability standard of the common law may have one other benefit for the media. It may in time improve the media's reputation for fairness and veracity with the general public because it will have a reason to believe in the accuracy of what is presented.

The substantive law of defamation, except in cases brought in the District of Columbia, is a matter of

state law. Thus, the extent to which the elimination of
Sullivan and its progeny from the scene as overriding
constitutional imperatives will result in a reversion to
common law rules of strict liability is not entirely
clear. States could elect to retain *Sullivan* on state
constitutional grounds, but this seems unlikely. The
damage limitation rules would, of course, apply to all
defamation actions. The proposed modifications of the
Federal Rules of Civil Procedure relating to special
verdicts, recovery of legal fees as costs, and offers of
judgment would apply only to actions in the Federal
Courts. It would be hoped that states would by judicial decision or statute follow the Supreme Court's
lead. Meanwhile, the hospitable provisions of the
Federal Rules of Civil Procedure may encourage
either party to bring or to remove the action to a
Federal Court whenever there is jurisdiction.

The present location of the balancing point
represents the Supreme Court's 1964 view of a
changed First Amendment imperative brought about
by conditions in existence at that time. By the simple
act of overruling *Sullivan*, the Court could restore the
pre-1964 state of First Amendment jurisprudence.
Using the First Amendment as the rationale, it could
further modify its *Gertz* holdings with respect to
measure and type of damages constitutionally
recoverable in libel actions. All of these could be done
by the Court on the same constitutional basis which
supported the *Sullivan* doctrine. After all, as one
English barrister has observed, "Constitutions are
made to be interpreted according to the needs of the
Times." (Robertson.)

This proposal will obviously not please those who

believe greater immunity for the press is the answer.
These commentators tend to attribute the over-
whelming trend of jury verdicts against the media to
lack of understanding of the law, bias against the
media, and reaction to unpopular ideas. (Franklin,
pp. 8-9.)

There is an alternative interpretation to be placed
on these data. It is that the law is inconsistent with the
public's perception of the proper balance between the
First Amendment and legal protection of reputation
and that the media is exercising its right under that
law in a way which the public deplores.

James Goodale, formerly General Counsel of the
New York Times, made these comments in 1983:

> "My own sense is that the public now harbors a
> great resentment against the press and it is show-
> ing up in jury verdicts in libel cases. . . . I think
> the public feels overwhelmed by a news medium
> that enters its home every night on television in
> living color, has the power to force an elected
> president to resign, and seems to be free from
> accountability. An easy way to get even with in-
> stituitions of this sort, which seems beyond the
> reach of ordinary Americans, is to vote huge libel
> verdicts against them." (*Id.*, p. 9, n. 42.)

The press is perceived as arrogant and reluctant to
admit its errors. "When 'ambush interviews,' the
practice of splicing separate questions and answers
together, and secret taping are added to scandals involving fabricated stories, it is not difficult to understand that the public may have doubts about the in-

tegrity and fairness of the media. Juries may well be manifesting general community resentment by imposing liability when given the opportunity."(*Id.*, pp. 9-10.)

The Tavoulareas case may provide an excellent example of this phenomenon. There, a jury had before it evidence that a reporter was chosen for the story whose nose had been publicly bloodied by a business associate of Tavoulareas; that the reporter approached the story as an opportunity to "knock off" the company which had humiliated him and of which Tavoulareas was President; that he discussed using felonious means to secure materials in Tavoulareas's possession; that he told customs officials a false story about Tavoulareas, presumably in an effort to generate more grist for his story mill; and, finally, that he promised a Congressman's assistant favorable publicity for the Congressman's letter to the SEC demanding an investigation of gossip and smears which the reporter had collected from sources he knew bore deep animosity toward Tavoulareas and, therefore, were unreliable. (Tavoulareas, *Fighting Back* [1985].) In the absence of any proof of out of pocket loss except legal fees of $1,800,000, the jury awarded Tavoulareas general damages of $250,000 and punitive damages of $1,800,000. (*Tavoulareas v. Washington Post*, 567 F. Supp. 651 [D.D.C. 1983].)

The School of Journalism and Mass Communication and the School of Law at the University of Iowa recently conducted a research project in the libel field which produced some pertinent findings. Among them were that the putative plaintiff has generally never filed a lawsuit before and does not want to sue, but is often impelled to do so. His first step is usually not to seek out an attorney, but to approach the media and seek a retraction. The treatment he receives in this process is so unpleasant that he then determines to file suit. (Assn. of the Bar Dissent, p. 72, n. 48.)

A former chief correspondent for Time and Life recently stated that

> "[M]any people feel the media have so much power that they should not easily take cover behind their unique constitutional shield. . . . [T]he press must change many of its ways. For example, if the media makes a serious factual charge against a public figure, they had better be able to offer proof that it is true. If they cannot . . . whether they believe it or not, they should retract the charge." (*Id.*, pp. 61-62, n. 21.)

Justice Potter Stewart in his concurring opinion in *Rosenblatt v. Baer* made the ultimate point in opposition to any rule of law which would permit the printing of lies with impunity by referring to the Senator McCarthy era:

> "[T]he rights and values of private personality far transcend mere personal interests. Surely if the 1950s taught us anything, they taught us that the poisonous atmosphere of the easy lie can infect and degrade a whole society." (383 U.S. 75, 93-94, 86 S.Ct. 669, 679-680 [1966].)

If our system will permit one deliberate liar to reach the United States Senate, who knows how many may reach the portals of power in the mighty media organizations of this country.

The public has a vital interest in the character and integrity of those individuals who aspire to positions of public trust and power. Should any group in the country be given the power to destroy the public's confidence in its leaders by the publication of deliberate falsehood? Put another way, it is the power to defraud the public out of its right to honest information about its leaders.

In England, the law has gone the other way, denying the fair comment privilege even to candidates for political office and applying strict liability defamation rules to their comments about each other. The belief is that public men, like private men, are entitled to the presumption of good reputation, and he who says otherwise should be prepared to prove it. It is hard to argue that that system produces less honorable men in public life than our system.

TOLERANCE

by

Andrew R. Cecil

Andrew R. Cecil

Andrew R. Cecil is Distinguished Scholar in Residence at The University of Texas at Dallas and Chancellor Emeritus and Honorary Trustee of The Southwestern Legal Foundation.

Associated with the Foundation since 1958, Dr. Cecil helped guide its development of five educational centers that offer nationally and internationally recognized programs in advanced continuing education.

In February 1979 the University established in his honor the Andrew R. Cecil Lectures on Moral Values in a Free Society, and invited Dr. Cecil to deliver the first series of lectures in November 1979. The first annual proceedings were published as Dr. Cecil's book The Third Way: Enlightened Capitalism and the Search for a New Social Order, *which received an enthusiastic response. He also lectured in each subsequent series. A new book,* The Foundations of a Free Society, *was published in 1983. Another,* Three Sources of National Strength, *appeared in 1986.*

Educated in Europe and well launched on a career as a professor and practitioner in the fields of law and economics, Dr. Cecil resumed his academic career after World War II in Lima, Peru, at the University of San Marcos. After 1949, he was associated with the Methodist church-affiliated colleges and universities in the United States until he joined the Foundation. He is author of twelve books on the subjects of law and economics and of more than seventy articles on these subjects and on the philosophy of religion published in periodicals and anthologies.

A member of the American Society of International Law, of the American Branch of the International Law Association, and the American Judicature Society, Dr. Cecil has served on numerous commissions for the Methodist Church, and is a member of the Board of Trustees of the National Methodist Foundation for Christian Higher Education. In 1981 he was named an Honorary Rotarian.

TOLERANCE

by

Andrew R. Cecil

Conflicting Views

In 1977 the American Nazi Party requested permission to hold a demonstration in Skokie, Illinois. The Circuit Court of Cook County, Illinois, issued an injunction barring the Nazis from "marching, walking or parading or otherwise displaying the swastika on or off their persons; [or] distributing pamphlets or displaying any materials which incite or promote hatred against persons of Jewish faith or ancestry or hatred against persons of any faith or ancestry, race or religion."

The Illinois Appellate Court held that the injunction was a restraint of activity protected by the First Amendment. The Court allowed the Nazis to demonstrate but did not allow the Nazis to display the swastika, since "the tens of thousands of Skokie Jewish residents must feel gross revulsion for the swastika and would immediately respond to the personally abusive epithets slung their way in the form of the defendant's chosen symbol, the swastika." (*Village of Skokie v. National Socialist Party of America*, 366 N.E. 2d 347 [1977].)

On January 27, 1978, the Illinois Supreme Court ruled that neither the swastika emblem nor the march

could be prohibited. The court took the position that
the swastika represents a symbolic act of speech that
conveys the beliefs of those who wear it. Therefore,
the display of the swastika, as offensive as it may be,
stated the court, cannot be precluded for the reason
that it may "provoke a violent reaction by those who
view it. Particularly this is true where, as here, there
has been advance notice by the demonstrators of their
plans . . . A speaker who gives prior notice of his
message has not compelled a confrontation with those
who voluntarily listen." The injunction was vacated.
The three new ordinances adopted by Skokie which
were intended to control demonstrations were
nullified as unconstitutional by the decision of the
Federal Court for the Northern District of Illinois,
affirmed by the Seventh Circuit Court of Appeals.
(*Collin v. Smith*, 578 F.2d. 1197, 7th Cir. [1978].)

No democracy can survive without freedom of
speech, which is the essence of tolerance. This
freedom, protected by the Constitution, is, however,
not absolute at all times and under all circumstances;
the lack of uniformity in the U.S. Supreme Court's interpretation of the law pertaining to inflammatory
speeches or action such as we have been discussing,
known as the "fighting words doctrine," is evidence of
this lack. Thus the U.S. Supreme Court has affirmed
the constitutionality of statutes that prohibit
obscenity or defamation and has affirmed the state's
power to punish an utterance directed at a defined
group, unless it is "a willful and purposeless restric-
tion unrelated to the peace and well being of the
State." (*Beauharnais v. Illinois*, 343 U.S. 250, 258, 72
S.Ct. 725, 731 [1952].)

In this case, Joseph Beauharnais, president of a fascist organization known as the White Circle League, was convicted for distributing in public places, in violation of the Illinois Criminal Code, leaflets portraying "depravity, criminality, unchastity or lack of virtue of citizens of Negro race and color." The Court in confirming the Illinois statutes referred to the tragic experience of the states that have been the scene of exacerbated tension between races, often flaring into violence and destruction. The Illinois legislature did have good reason, stated the Court, to seek ways to curb malicious defamation of racial and religious groups, made in public places and by means calculated to incite violence and breaches of the peace.

Such transgressions the states may punish appropriately. The Court found unconvincing the argument that the choice the Supreme Court opened to legislatures may be abused and can be only a step away from prohibiting libel of a political party. Every power may be abused, and the possibility of abuse is a poor reason for denying the state legislature the right to adopt measures against criminal libels "sanctioned by centuries of Anglo-American law."

The same position was taken by the U.S. Supreme Court in the case of *Chaplinsky v. New Hampshire*. Chaplinsky, a member of the sect known as Jehovah's Witnesses, while proselytizing on the streets of Rochester, New Hampshire, denounced all religions as a "racket." When arrested for disturbing the peace, he insulted the city marshal by calling him "a damned fascist" and a "goddamned racketeer." The Court, following the "fighting words" doctrine, found that Chaplinsky's utterances were not "an essential part of any exposition of ideas" and were "of such slight social value as a step to truth that any benefit that may be derived from them is clearly outweighed by the social interests in order and morality." The Court unanimously affirmed a conviction based on a statute of the state of New Hampshire that banned speeches that could inflict injury or an immediate breach of the peace. (315 U.S. 568, 572, 62 S.Ct. 766, 769 [1942].)

An analysis of the meaning of violence we find in the position adopted by the Supreme Court that advocacy of violence merely used as a means of accomplishing political reform is constitutionally protected and should be distinguished from advocacy of violence intended to incite imminent unlawful conduct. (*Brandenburg v. Ohio*, 395 U.S. 444, 446, 89 S.Ct. 1827, 1829 [1969].) In this case, Brandenburg, a leader of the Ku Klux Klan convicted under an Ohio Criminal Syndicalism statute, stated: "We are not a revengent organization, but if our President, our Congress, our Supreme Court, continues to suppress the white caucasian race, it's possible that there might have to be some revengeance taken." The Court reversed the conviction because the constitutionality of the Criminal Syndicalism Act could not be sustained; it makes no distinction between mere advocacy of violence from preparing a group for violent action and steeling it to such action.

The United States Supreme Court took a similar position in the *Terminiello v. City of Chicago* case. The Court overturned a "breach of the peace" conviction based on an ordinance of the city of Chicago, which as construed by the trial court included in "breach of the peace" any speech which "stirs the public to anger, incites dispute, brings about a condition of unrest, or creates a disturbance . . ." In this case, a suspended Catholic priest named Terminiello, in an address delivered in an auditorium in Chicago under the auspices of the Christian Veterans of America, criticized various racial and political groups whose activities he denounced as inimical to the nation's welfare. At the meeting, he hurled at the inflamed mob of his adversaries such epithets as "slimy scum," "snakes," "bedbugs," and the like. Disturbances caused by a turbulent and angry crowd ensued. The convictions for "breach of the peace" were affirmed by both the Illinois Appellate and the Illinois Supreme Courts.

The United States Supreme Court reversed the conviction because parts of the Chicago ordinance were unconstitutional. The function of free speech, stated the Court, "is to invite dispute. It may indeed best serve its high purpose when it induces a condition of unrest, creates dissatisfaction with conditions as they are, or even stirs people in anger . . . That is why freedom of speech, though not absolute, . . . is nevertheless protected against censorship or punishment, unless shown likely to produce a *clear and present danger of a serious substantive evil that rises far above public inconvenience, annoyance, or unrest.*" (337 U.S. 1, 4, 69 S.Ct. 894, 896 [1949] Emphasis added.)

The apparent contradictions in the decisions of the Courts which we have been discussing raises a number of questions: Is there a constitutional obligation to tolerate groups or individuals who advocate violence or who deride or discredit a class of citizens of a certain creed, religion, race, or color? What kind of unrest and disturbance must violence create in order to rise "far above public inconvenience, annoyance, or unrest" and to justify the employment of the "clear and present danger" provision of the violence test? Are not outbreaks of violence, lynching, or rioting as a rule incited by hatred and passion supplied by speeches to some mass of people? What restraint should be placed on the extent of tolerance of actions that advocate a resort to force and violence so as to preserve a balance between tolerance and other values which are essential for democracies to function properly, including freedom of speech, freedom of the press, freedom of worship, and other fundamental personal rights and liberties? Are there rules and procedures democracies should pursue to keep violent tendencies in check? Where is the real defense line?

A Definition of Tolerance

In order to answer these questions, it will be helpful to define the concept of tolerance and to outline a brief history of its development. Tolerance derives from the Latin *tolerantia*, a term intended to give the notion of bearing without repugnance, of enduring or putting up with. The term "tolerance" presupposes opposition or objection to a certain idea, behavior, or thing, and its ultimate acceptance. It reflects a self-restraint that permits us to reconcile our disapproval of certain opinions and practices with our acceptance of the right of others to pursue them. Such acceptance is not a sign of weakness. It suggests an attitude of putting up with people, not of giving in to them.

This self-restraint represents a concession and not always an absence of prejudice. A prejudiced person can be tolerant when he checks his impulses, blocks any action based upon his objection, and accepts the things toward which he is prejudiced. A businessman may be prejudiced against a certain minority group but be tolerant in his employment policies by constraining his prejudice and by not permitting himself to translate his negative attitude into discrimination.

Tolerance should not be confused with indifference. While tolerance reflects genuine disagreement, indifference marks absence of compulsion, interest, or concern about something. Lack of concern, for instance, whether a group claiming to be a religious sect or its leaders are engaged in fraudulent activities or are worshipping according to the beliefs of its members, is not tolerance but a socially harmful attitude. Such an attitude reflects neither a real objection to nor a real acceptance of the right to exist—the two prerequisites of tolerance.

Intolerance

Tolerance of intolerance aggravates intolerance. There are those who invoke tolerance as part of a strategy of overthrowing democracy, with which tolerance is closely associated as one of its fundamental principles. In our times, an appeal for tolerance has been used by fascists and communists in their efforts to destroy democracy. Goebbels stated: "When democracy granted democratic methods for us in times of opposition, this [Nazi seizure of power] was bound to happen in a democratic system. However, we National Socialists never asserted that we represented a democratic point of view, but we have declared openly that we used democratic methods only in order to gain the power and that, after assuming the power, we would deny to our adversaries without any consideration the means which were granted to us in times of (our) opposition." (1 Nazi Conspiracy & Aggression [GPO 1946] 202, Docs. 2500-PS, 2412-PS.)

Similarly, the communists continue to claim that their right to convey their political ideas in our country is protected by the First Amendment, and consequently they have the right to give speeches, engage in demonstrations, and advocate in their publications the overthrow of our duly elected government by force. History shows that, once they succeed in destroying an organized free society, the dictatorship they offer means, according to Lenin, "nothing more nor less than completely unrestricted power, absolutely unimpeded by laws or regulations and resting directly on the use of force." With the destruction of a free society, they destroy all civil liberties and the security of freedom enjoyed in a democratic State. The diabolical outrages against human personality thus perpetrated are motivated by the fact that the "solidarity and the internal unity of the Party" cannot afford "to be too liberal or permit freedom of factions." (Joseph Stalin, *Problems of Leninism*, Foreign Language Publishing House, Moscow, 1952, p. 175.)

In maintaining a democratic policy of political tolerance we must recognize that intolerance of intolerance safeguards tolerance. The foundation of a democratic system is endangered if there is no protection against the excesses of unrestrained abuses committed by those who advocate the adoption of communism or another form of totalitarian regime. They use or enhance mob violence, race rioting, and all kinds of public disorders in order to suppress—once they come to power—our liberties. The choice is not between tolerance and order. It is between tolerance with order and anarchy without order. Adherence to the doctrinaire logic that civil liberty means removal of all restraints may convert the constitutional guarantees on which our democracy is based into a suicide pact.

History demonstrates that tolerance of intolerance is suicidal for civil liberties and human rights. We can hardly be reminded too often that there was a Socrates who devoted himself to the intellectual and moral improvement of the Athenians by spending his life talking wherever men congregated about justice, knowledge, piety, and other moral values. When Athens was ruined by the Peloponnesian War, Socrates was sacrificed by the bigotry of the city, which made him responsible for the collapse of the Athenian virtues. When brought to trial, he was convicted for impiety, immorality, and corruption of youth and was condemned to drink the poison hemlock. Socrates, one of the most eminent thinkers in the history of mankind, was put to death as a criminal.

Religious Intolerance

Reinhold Niebuhr wrote that "the worst form of intolerance is religious intolerance, in which the particular interests of the contestants hide behind religious absolutes." (*The Nature and Destiny of Man*, Vol. I, Charles Scribner's Sons, 1941, pp. 200-210.)

The history of the organized church teems with instances of intolerance and persecution of religious movements against the authority and the worldly interests of the church. Religious toleration was condemned as a heresy. Religious intolerance asserted itself externally in crusades or holy wars and internally in persecution. In one holy war, for instance, Charlemagne gave the Saxons and the Bohemians the choice between baptism and death. With fire and sword he carried the Gospel of the Cross down to the Adriatic coast and drove the Moslems back from the Pyrenees as far as Barcelona.

As for those who dissented within the church, "heretics" were executed—burned to death and hanged. Catholics as well as early Protestants persecuted dissident sects mercilessly. The twelfth-century monk Arnold de Brescia, who advocated the idea that possession of property was an exclusive right of lay powers and that the church had no right to hold property, was tried and executed by the Roman Curia. The Italian Dominican friar Savonarola (1452-1498), who preached against the corruption of society and predicted the forthcoming punishment of the church and its regeneration, was hanged by the Florentine government after it had forced him to confess that he was not a prophet.

John Wycliff, whose translation of the Bible was an important landmark in the history of English literature, was condemned twice as a heretic for spreading the doctrine that the Scriptures are the supreme authority. He was the forerunner of the Reformation, and in 1419 the Pope ordered the burning of his books. Huss, the Bohemian religious reformer and the leading opponent of the condemnation of Wycliff's writings, at the invitation of Emperor Sigismund and under the protection of the emperor's safe-conduct, presented himself at the Council of Constance, only to be imprisoned, tried, and burned at the stake as a heretic.

In 1616 the Copernican theory of the solar system was denounced by the Church as dangerous to faith. When Galileo, the great Italian astronomer and physicist, in his *Dialogue of the Two Chief Systems of the World* of 1632 confirmed the acceptance of the Copernican theory, he was tried by the Inquisition and obliged to abjure the "error" in his belief that the sun is the central body and the earth with the other planets revolves around it. His indefinite imprisonment was only ended by Pope Urban VIII.

Just as the Catholics used execution as a means to wipe out "heresy," so the early Protestants thought that any opposition to their religious practices implied evil that had to be eradicated. Michael Servetus, the Spanish physician and theologian (1511-1553), was condemned by Calvin for his antitrinitarian writings.

By Calvin's order he was seized in Geneva, and after a long trial was burned at the stake on October 27, 1553. Like the Catholics, the early Protestants believed that if a man remained outside their faith he was condemned to burn forever in hell, and therefore he should be compelled even by torture to change his beliefs by force. Such conversion was deemed to save his soul and provide him with eternal life.

The leaders of the church in the Middle Ages, advocating persecution for religious nonconformity, argued that they were acting in accordance with Christ's commandment, "Go out on the highways and hedgerows and make them come in." (Luke 14:23.) The literal interpretation of this commandment (*compelle intrare*—"make them come in") was attributed to St. Augustine; it justified intolerance and forced conversion. When torture was used as a means of conversion, the leaders of the church maintained, the pain caused by forced coercion was nothing to what heretics and schismatics would suffer in hell, where men who remain outside the faith are condemned to burn forever. If a man died in the process of torture, at least he was rewarded with eternal life.

Religious Toleration

In the sixteenth and seventeenth centuries, a concern for religious toleration arose, and in the nineteenth and twentieth centuries, a similar concern for political tolerance grew up. (We use both the terms "toleration" and "tolerance." "Toleration" is identified with religion, while the term "tolerance" applies to political controversies. The modern concept of tolerance has its origin in religious "toleration," but both types of tolerance—or toleration—reflect opposition to intolerance.) Starting with the sixteenth century, numerous writers saw in ecclesiastical power and forcible conversion the root of intolerance and came to realize that in a healthy society men have to tolerate one another's political, religious, and philosophical differences. We shall briefly review the ideas of two brilliant representatives of this Age of Enlightenment, of this age of Reason and Knowledge—F.M.A. de Voltaire and John Locke. Both of them were greatly influenced by French philosopher Pierre Bayle (1647-1706), the Huguenot author of the *Traité de la tolerance universelle*, published in 1686.

Bayle believed that each person has the untrammeled and unquestionable right to worship God according to the dictates of his own conscience. Persecution or attempts to coerce a person to worship God in a particular way, stated Bayle, will never result in conviction, but will only produce hypocrites or martyrs. (He tolerated the atheist but denied, however, the right of religious liberty to the Catholic church, which should not in his judgment be tolerated because it actively and persistently promoted intolerance.) Forced conversion, according to Bayle, could not be reconciled with Christ's commandments of love for our fellowman, charity, forgiveness, and respect for human dignity. It is a sacrilegious offense to God Himself.

The tolerance advocated by Bayle was based on the principle of doubt concerning the substance of truth. To him it appeared impossible to define or to know with certainty "que la Verité que nous paroit est la

Verité absolue"—that the truth that appears to us is
the absolute truth. Bayle's position reminds us that
when Jesus was asked by Pontius Pilate whether He
was a king, He replied, "My task is to bear witness to
the truth. For this was I born; for this I came into the
world, and all who are not deaf to truth listen to my
voice." Scholars have not yet agreed to a definition of
what this truth is.

Because of this uncertainty and the commitment to
search for the substance of truth, Bayle believed that
"la Religion est une affaire du conscience, qui ne se
commande pas"—religion is a matter of conscience
which cannot be ordered. The Bible, as well as
the above-mentioned principle "compelle intrare,"
should be interpreted in accordance with "la Lumière
Naturelle"—natural reason, which rejects forced conversion and commands religious toleration because of
the difficulty of ascertaining the nature of truth. He
believed that Christians, Jews, and Moslems should
enjoy mutual religious toleration because no one can
claim absolute knowledge of God's commands and of
the ultimate mysteries of the universe. As to the
Augustinian justification of using constraint, Bayle
wrote, "What matters is not to which end constraint is
used, but whether it is used at all."

Religion and Superstition

François-Marie Voltaire, the eighteenth century
French philosopher and author, in his encyclopedia
(which he called a *Philosophic Dictionary*) thanked
Bayle for familiarizing him with the art of doubt.
Educated by Jesuits in the art of dialectic, of proving

anything, he stated, "I have taken as my patron saint St. Thomas of Didymus, who always insisted on an examination with his own hands." As an illustration of Voltaire's application of the "art of doubt," one of his works (which fill ninety-nine volumes) may serve—the pamphlet called "The Questions of Zapata," in which Zapata, a candidate for the priesthood, asks: "How shall we proceed to show that the Jews, whom we burn by the hundred, were for four thousand years the chosen people of God?"

Voltaire, detesting intolerance and superstition, stressed the fundamental distinction between religion and superstition. In his articles on "God" and "Theist" in the *Dictionary*, he defends religion and expounds his faith in the existence of a supreme being "who has formed all things" and "who punishes without cruelty all crimes, and recompenses with goodness all virtuous actions." Religion, he argued, should not be confused with superstition, which he described as the "cruelest enemy of pure worship due to the Supreme Being," as "a monster which has always torn the bosom of its mother," and as "a serpent which chokes religion in its embrace" that must have its head crushed "without wounding the mother whom it devours."

In his later life Voltaire, hostile to religious dogmatism, expended more and more of his effort to combat intolerance and injustice. The Calas case was one of the events that provoked him to his crusade to "crush the infamy" of ecclesiasticism and intolerance (he used the motto *Ecrasez l'infame* to end all his letters) by waging a relentless war against superstition, corruption, and abuses of the church. The Catholic church in his time enjoyed absolute sovereignty, and Voltaire's famous fight to secure justice for the family of Jean Calas of Toulouse, a victim of religious persecution, stirred the soul of France, if not of Europe, on behalf of tolerance, liberty, and humanity.

Jean Calas, who followed the profession of a merchant in Toulouse for over forty years, was known as a good parent and a respected citizen. He, his wife, and all his children (one son, Louis Calas, excepted) were Protestants. For thirty years, a maid-servant, a zealous Catholic, brought up all his children. One of his sons, Marc-Antonio, who could not as a Protestant enter into business nor be admitted to the bar as a lawyer, hanged himself—presumably because of the disappointments he had experienced. When the people of Toulouse gathered in crowds about the house, some fanatic in the mob cried out that Jean Calas had hanged his own son. In consequence, a rumor started in Toulouse—a city that celebrated by annual procession and bonfire the Massacre of St. Bartholomew (when four thousand Huguenots were massacred as heretics)—that the father had killed the son to prevent his imminent conversion to Catholicism.

Calas was arrested and sentenced to be broken on the wheel. His son Pierre was shut up in a monastery of Dominicans; the daughters were taken from their mother and shut up in a convent. The daughters wre restored to their mother only after three famous lawyers took up the widow's cause. Voltaire, in his "Treatise on Tolerance," concludes the account of the daath of Jean Calas by pointing out that "the abuse of the most holy religion has produced a great crime. It is therefore to the interest of mankind to examine if religion should be charitable or savage." The Calas case was only one of the tyrannous injustices resulting from fanaticism composed of superstition and ignorance that Voltaire opposed.

In the article on "Tolerance" in his *Philosophical Dictionary*, Voltaire asks why the same men who in private admit indulgence, benevolence, and justice, in public rise up so furiously against these virtues? Because, he maintains, men who "enrich themselves with the spoils of the poor, fatten themselves with his blood, and laugh at his imbecility . . . detest tolerance, as contractors enriched at the expense of the public are afraid to open their accounts, and as tyrants dread the name of liberty."

Although, according to Voltaire, Christians have been the most intolerant of all men, he nevertheless believed that of all religions, "the Christian ought doubtless to inspire the most tolerance." Because of the horrible discord experienced by mankind for so many centuries, Voltaire appealed for mutual forgiveness because "discord is the great evil of the human species, and toleration is its only remedy." He defined tolerance as "the portion of humanity" and as "the first law of nature."

Separation of Government from Church

John Locke (1632-1704), the English philosopher called the "founder of British Empiricism" who greatly influenced Voltaire, proclaimed toleration as "the chief characteristic mark of the Church." He, like

Voltaire, believed that freedom of religion is a natural right that neither any single person, nor churches, nor governments have any just title to invade. He wrote three essays in favor of religious toleration. In his *A Letter Concerning Toleration*, Locke appealed to the conscience of those who upon pretense of religion persecute, destroy, starve, and maim men with corporal punishment to make them Christians and procure their salvation. Nobody will ever believe, he maintained, that such torments can proceed from charity, love, and goodwill. This "burning zeal for God," stated Locke, is "contrary to the glory of God, to the purity of the Church" and is "diametrically opposite to the profession of Christianity."

The only remedy, according to Locke, to put an end to controversy is the separation of civil government from the church. The interest of men's souls should be distinguished from the interest of the commonwealth. Religion is a matter of faith, and the nature of faith is that it cannot be compelled to the belief of anything by outward force. The power of true religion consists "in the inward and full persuasion of the mind, and faith is not faith without believing." God has never given the authority to take care of souls to one man over another or to compel anyone to his religion. Locke went a step further by stating that such power cannot be vested in the state even by the consent of the people, because no man can abandon the care of his own salvation. No man can leave the choice of his faith to any other, and "no man can prescribe to another what faith or worship he shall embrace."

Locke argued that nobody is born a member of any

church. Since the church is "a society of members voluntarily uniting to that end," joining the church should be absolutely free and spontaneous. The only business of the church, according to Locke, is the salvation of souls. No one can be saved by a religion he distrusts or by worship he abhors. "Faith only, and inward sincerity, are the things that procure acceptance with God." Imposition of religion upon any people contrary to their own judgment "is in effect to command them to offend God. . . ." If we are not fully satisfied in our own mind with the worship to which we conform, we add to other sins "those also of hypocrisy, and contempt of His Divine Majesty." The ecclesiastical authority of the Church ought to be confined within its bounds, and it cannot in any manner be extended to civil affairs, "because the Church itself is a thing absolutely separate and distinct from the commonwealth."

The "commonwealth" is defined by Locke as "a society of men constituted only for processing, preserving, and advancing their own civil interests." The civil interests include, life, liberty, and property. The civil power of the government ("the magistrate") is confined to the care of promoting the "civil interests," and it cannot and ought not in any manner be extended to the salvation of souls. Princes, wrote Locke, are "born superior unto other men in power, but in nature equal." Therefore, neither the right nor the art of ruling carries with it the knowledge of true religion. Thus, like Bayle and Voltaire, Locke introduces the principle of uncertainty about true religion as fundamental to the promotion of religious toleration.

Religious tolerance, stated Locke, does not permit the government to prejudice any man in the enjoyment of his civil rights because of his religion. All his civil rights and franchises that belong to him are inviolably preserved to him. "No violence nor injury is to be offered him, whether he be Christian or Pagan." Since the power of civil government relates only to men's civil rights, it is confined "to the care of the things of this world, and hath nothing to do with the world to come." In other words, the boundaries on both sides, on the side of the church as well as on the side of the state, are fixed and immovable.

Political Tolerance

The influence of Locke was exceedingly great. It spread widely in eighteenth century Europe, and it has been asserted that all the philosophy of that century stemmed from him. Locke's ideas on natural law contributed to the beginning of a new social and economic system that reflected the meaning of newborn ideas of freedom of religion and of thought and of a government limited in its powers and based firmly on consent. Locke's conception of a fiduciary relation between free individuals and rulers with the duties of the government as trustee and with the rights of the community as beneficiary was appealing to those who struggled for the preservation of the independence, freedom, and equality with which individuals are endowed by nature.

Locke's conception of religious tolerance, based on the separation of church and state and on the religious freedom of the individual, was a landmark in the history of relations between government and the church, which in England from the time of the Tudors had backed the claims of monarchy. His doctrine of the separation of powers, although not formulated as clearly as by Montesquieu or as by modern practice (which places the legislative, executive, and judicial functions in distinct hands, while Locke's thought permitted combining them), and his doctrine of consent between government and society were the main sources of the English Revolution of 1688 (the so-called "Glorious Revolution"), of the ideas that underlay the American Revolution of 1776, and of the traditions of political tolerance that emerged in the nineteenth and twentieth centuries. This tradition of political tolerance made possible the rise of the modern political party.

The system of governance through political parties arose in Great Britain, beginning in the seventeenth century. The oppositions which gave birth to the parties were initially religious. The Anglicans, who favored the Established church and supported the power of the king, grew into the Tory party. The Dissenters, Protestants who belonged to sects other than the Established church and who upheld the power of the Parliament, were labeled Whigs. These divisions were often social and economic as well. The Tories were stronger in rural areas and were favored by the country gentlemen. The Whigs, more numerous in urban areas, tended to be strong among the new mercantile middle class.

Although the British parties first arose in the seventeenth century, these distinctions continued to be important throughout subsequent British political history. After the French Revolution, the Whig party espoused political and social reforms that culminated in the passage of the Reform Bill of 1832. About that time, the name "Tory" gave way to "Conservative," and the name "Whig" to "Liberal." In the era of Benjamin Disraeli, his followers called themselves "young Tories" and ultraconservatives were referred to as Tories. In the twentieth century, the line of division between the Tories and the Whigs became outmoded and gave way to new groupings of contestants. The two principal parties of today are the Conservative party (which like the Tories appeals to the gentry and the upper middle class) and the Labor party (which appeals to organized labor and the lower middle class). Minor third parties may on occasion hold the balance of powers.

As the parties first arose, their coexistence was not based on ideas of political tolerance. Nor was that coexistence a peaceful one. The execution of King Charles I, the reign of his son Charles II after the Restoration of the monarchy (marked by a gradual increase in parliamentary power and the rise of political parties), and the so-called Glorious Revolution of 1688 (in which James II, who succeeded his brother Charles II, was forced to abdicate in favor of his daughter Mary and her husband, William) were all tremendous upheavals in an age fraught with religious plotting and violence. These successive upheavals were only in part caused by a fear of the monarchs' leaning toward Catholicism, a religion which neither of the incipient parties was willing to tolerate officially.

The ultimate issue was the supremacy in government of either the King or Parliament. Charles I (1600-1649), who lost the bitter struggle with the Parliament, was tried, condemned to death, and beheaded. This struggle, known as the Puritan Revolution, marked the emergence of the middle class—the new bourgeois class, Calvinist by inclination. This group perennially suspected the monarchy of having plans to restore Roman Catholicism in England, and finally these suspicions were brought to a head by James II. He was deposed without bloodshed in 1688 (in the Glorious Revolution, so named because of its peacefulness in contradistinction to the Puritan Revolution, with its warlike violence and its regicide). The joint coronation of William and Mary to replace James II ultimately established the supremacy of Parliament in the English government.

Political Parties

The party system, however, did not become a decisive part of government in Great Britain until the nineteenth century, when Parliament—by then representing a much more widely enfranchised electorate—gained final ascendancy over the monarch as the ruling body of the nation. Each party became an organized body within itself, with an internal structure and an effective means of disciplining its members into a cohesive group within Parliament. (Party discipline in Great Britain is much stronger than in the United States, where legislators seldom vote strictly along party lines except for purposes of organizing the houses of Congress and their Committees).

One British historian pointed out the relationship between the British party system and the tradition of political tolerance which underpins the British system of government:

> "Tolerance in this country is a principle of long standing. It has developed gradually from the struggles of the seventeenth century. It has been carried out in the laws; but it is still more an attitude of mind. It is, however, not tolerance alone that makes democratic government work. With us, the majority is not permanent. . . . Majorities are unstable, and the Opposition of today is the Government of tomorrow. This important fact must not be forgotten, for it enables the minority to submit peacefully and even cheerfully to the fulfillment of the policy of the majority." (W. Ivor Jennings, *The British Constitution*, Cambridge University Press, 1942, pp. 32-33.)

The important part of the British system of government referred to as "His (or Her) Majesty's Opposition" dramatizes the need for tolerance of diverse opinions. In the seventeenth century, it was the function of the Parliament to oppose the King. Now it is the function of "His Majesty's Opposition" to oppose the governmental majority. The Leader of the opposition has a shadow Cabinet that formulates a rival policy to that of the government in power. He has a salary paid from public funds included in each year's appropriation. The opposition, which always presents the electorate with the possibility of an alternative government, is as loyal as the government in power to the British system of government. In both World Wars, for instance, it shared responsibility by becoming a part of the wartime coalition governments. At the end of the wars, the coalitions broke up, and the political parties appealed for the voters of the electorate. Even under normal circumstances, the government in power in Great Britain must take into account the views of the opposition, which functions together with the majority government as guardians of the British tradition of parliamentary government.

Jefferson's Impact on Tolerance

Locke, as we mentioned, had an impact not only on the British system of government but also on the ideals of the American Revolution of 1776. He greatly influenced Thomas Jefferson, and the infusion of the idea of natural rights with the spirit of natural law found its expression in our Declaration of Independence. Jefferson, like Locke, believed that "man, being the workmanship of the omnipotent and infinitely wise Maker," has rights on his own to freedom of religion. The importance of religious tolerance in the United States may be traced back to Jefferson's defense of religious freedom. In his *Notes on Virginia*, 1782, Jefferson wrote:

> "Reason and free enquiry are the only effectual agents against error . . . It is error alone which needs the support of government. Truth can stand

by itself . . . Difference of opinion is advantageous in religion . . . Is uniformity attainable? Millions of innocent men, women and children since the introduction of Christianity have been burnt, tortured, fined, imprisoned. Yet have we not advanced one inch towards uniformity. What has been the effect of coercion? To make one half the world fools and the other half hypocrites. To support roguery and error all over the earth . . ."

Jefferson saw in reason and free inquiry "the natural enemies of error" and was determined to destroy the alliance between the church and the state as the barrier to free inquiry and as the enemy of personal freedom. This determination was supported by the peace and order enjoyed by the states of Pennsylvania and New York that had long subsisted without an establishment of state religion at all. The result of this experiment, witnessed by Jefferson, was not religious dissension, but an unparalleled harmony that could be ascribed to nothing but the "unbounded tolerance" of these two states that silenced religious disputes.

To protect his fellow citizens in Virginia from coercion in matters of conscience and to proclaim their right to worship as they chose, Jefferson drafted a Bill for Establishing Religious Freedom that advocated full religious liberty. Following the sweeping declaration that Almighty God had created man free and that all attempts to influence him by punishment tend "only to beget habits of hypocrisy" and are departures "from the plan of the holy author of our religion," the Bill provided

"that no man shall be compelled to frequent or
support any religious worship, place, or ministry
whatsoever, nor shall be enforced, restrained,
molested, or burthened in his body or goods, nor
shall otherwise suffer on account of his religious
opinions or beliefs but that all men shall be free to
profess, and by argument to maintain, their
opinions in matters of religion, and that the same
shall in no wise diminish, enlarge, or affect their
civil capacities . . ."

Because of the opposition of the General Assembly
of Virginia, the Bill waited several years for passage.
When at last it had been approved, Jefferson, who
was at that time in France, wrote to Madison, "It is
honorable for us to have produced the first legislation
which had the courage to declare that the reason of
man may be trusted with the formation of his
opinions."

Locke's influence was not confined to ideas of
religious tolerance. Into the political texture of
American life are interwoven the ideas of English con-
stitutionalism of which Locke was a prominent
spokesman. Our republican type of representative
democracy was created in the image of the English
representative ideal, to which Locke had given expression, claiming that "The end of government is the
good of mankind." This type of democracy provided a
climate for the cultivation of political tolerance, but
the distinctive source of political tolerance in the
United States was the unity and the identity of
purposes of the early settlers who came to America
with the aim of building a society that would offer its

members equality of opportunity with little political control. This identity of purpose embraced both conservatives and liberals. Moreover, the tradition of tolerance was indispensable in order to accomplish another unique purpose of the American experiment in establishing equality in freedom: to stimulate similar aspirations of other nations.

Jefferson, in his belief that the "eyes of the virtuous all over the earth are turned with anxiety on us, as the only depositories of the sacred fire of liberty," saw in "a just and solid republican government . . . a standing monument and example for the aim and imitation of the people of other countries." On a similar note President Lincoln stressed that the Declaration of Independence gave liberty "not alone to the people of this country, but hope to the world for all future time." Only political tolerance could guarantee that America would never become an image of Europe, where intolerance under the pretext of public safety was a tool used by corrupted governments to enhance the heresy that man is incapable of self-government.

Opposing Political Ideas

Tolerance, which constituted the fundamental prerequisite for the success of the American experiment, did not imply conformity of thought and of the conceptions concerning national purpose and the ways to acheive it. Tolerance permitted the expression of diametrically opposed political ideas. We shall mention only two such contradictory conceptions. One related to foreign policy: Charles Pinckney (1746-1825), the American statesman and diplomat,

declared on January 25, 1787, at the Federal Convention, of which he was a member, that "we mistake the
object of our government, if we hope or wish it is to
make us respectable abroad." Following the Greek
philosophers, he saw the purpose of the new nation in
the good life, in which foreign policy could largely be
neglected. Alexander Hamilton represented an
opposite point of view when on June 29 of the same
year he declared, "No Government could give us
tranquility and happiness at home, which did not
possess sufficient stability and strength to make
us respectable abroad." Hamilton followed the
European tradition that expected the government to
obtain not only domestic tranquility but also respecta-
bility in the eyes of foreign nations.

One of the controversies as old as American politics
was the argument of a strong versus a weak federal
government. The two contrasting political groups
were represented by Jefferson and Hamilton. Both
were openly antagonistic members of Washington's
Cabinet, and Washington was unable to reconcile
them. Jefferson, born of the highest aristocracy of
Virginia, had a passionate love of liberty and a faith in
the people's capacity for self-government. In his zeal
as an apostle of agrarian democracy, Jefferson saw his
ideal in a community of independent families solidly
established in their farms, self-subsistent and needing
little or no interference. "Those who labor in the
earth are the chosen people of God, if ever he had a
chosen people." A strong centralized government by
its nature could endanger liberty. Hamilton, a self-
made man in the fullest sense, saw in the federal
government an indispensable tool for an ordered

society and for the collective interests of the people. He and James Madison provided the leadership in securing the adoption of the Constitution.

Jefferson saw in government a horde of office-holders dominated by greed and corruption, depriving free individuals of the fruits of their labor on their God-given land in this blessed country of the United States. Hamilton did not find in Jefferson's faith in the free expression of the individual an assurance of man's capacity to deal on his own with the conflicting interests arising in a society without some kind of direction in public affairs, which only a government with a strong central authority can provide. He feared that a weak government would lead to disunion and anarchy.

The opposing philosophies of the two men have continued to influence the political history of the United States. Hamilton was the recognized leader of those who favored the Constitution and who called themselves the Federalists. The Anti-Federalists, who earned this name because they fought desperately against the ratification of the Constitution, feared that the Constitution would provide too strong and too centralized a government. With the loss of the battle, in order to restrict the powers of the new national government, they chose their own interpretation of the Constitution, accepted Jefferson as their leader, and identified themselves as Jeffersonian Republicans. Their aim was to destroy forever the possibility of a monarchy or of an aristocratic government. Acting as champions for the oppressed, they advocated a wider distribution of wealth, thus gaining strength among the destitute immigrants arriving in this country.

The Republicans were the origin of the present Democratic party. (The irony is that President Reagan became the modern promulgator of antigovernmental Jeffersonianism.) Jefferson did not call himself either a Federalist or an anti-Federalist. He was anxious to preserve the unity and cooperation of the new government and claimed, "We are all Republicans, we are all Federalists."

There was animosity between Jefferson and Hamilton and their followers. They became openly antagonistic, but both of them shared the same passion—they loved their country above all things. When in the presidential election Aaron Burr was found to have tied in number of votes with Jefferson, the choice of a President was thrown into the House of Representatives. After a long deadlock, Jefferson was elected, largely because Hamilton advised Federalists to support Jefferson. This election marked a historical triumph of political tolerance. For the first time in the modern era, the reins of the government were peacefully transferred by popular election from a governing party (the Federalists with President John Adams retiring from public life) to an opposition (Jefferson and his Republicans).

The System of Party Government

The party system in the United States grew indirectly out of the British experience in the eighteenth century. In the colonial period, the early

Americans were divided, as in Britain, into two opposed groups, the Tories and the Whigs. The first favored the crown and represented the merchants, large landowners, and commercial creditors. The Whigs advocated home rule and voiced the sentiments of the indebted inland farmers. The conflicting interests of opposing groups did not imply a two-party system. The Federalists, for instance, saw themselves as defenders of the Constitution and not as a party. Similarly, Jefferson's attitude toward the party system was characteristic of that of other early American leaders; he profoundly distrusted party politics and was uncomfortable in admitting the role party actually came to play in American political life, even in its earliest years. For John Adams, our first vice president, the division of the Republic into two great parties "is to be feared as the greatest political evil under the Constitution." The frequent splits and formation of new parties did not enhance the popularity of a party system.

Even in spite of the fact that the Founding Fathers looked with mistrust at the party system, the United States evolved a system of party government that has been one of the bulwarks of liberty in the nation. One of the principal qualities developed by the party system in the United States, as in Great Britain, is the atmosphere of mutual tolerance, resulting in the tradition of responsible opposition engaged in a legitimate activity, and of adherence to the rules of constitutional procedure and of fairness. The spirit of political tolerance is sustained in years of election when the political chips are piled high and the

campaigns tend to inflame the participants. No punitive action is taken by the winners against those who
opposed them. Any attempt to transcend the bounds
of what is legal, moral, and civil will turn the
momentum in favor of the opposition.

In the United States, the common belief in political
tolerance is strengthened by the common ground on
which the two parties stand. Neither of the two political parties has a doctrinaire set of principles that stand
in fierce opposition to those of the other party. The
lines of distinction between the platforms of the two
parties are not clearly drawn. No meaningful
differences are to be found in the ultimate goals
sought by the two parties. The distinction rather
appears in the role assigned by the parties to the
government in achieving those goals. The Democrats
have a tendency to use the government for furnishing
social services on a wider scale than the Republicans,
who place greater faith in private initiative and in the
individual's ability to shape his destiny. Bipartisan
consensus often reflects the general agreement on a
broad range of issues in foreign policy and other important matters faced by our nation.

In a time of crisis in the United States, for instance,
the President will usually invite to the White House
the Congressional leaders of both parties to inform
them of the situation at hand and to seek their advice
and cooperation. At the moments of greatest importance, the cooperation is often greatest. In 1948,
for instance, when the United States was embarking
on the then-momentous step of entering into the
North American Treaty Organization (NATO), it was a

Republican Senator, Arthur H. Vandenberg, who in-
troduced into the Congress the resolution that made
it possible for the Democratic President Harry S.
Truman, to pursue the ends of the treaty. Although
the lack of clear party lines and strong party discipline
in our country may be somehow confusing, it is a
pattern that has served well to prevent the more
doctrinaire multiparty system and to accept tolerance
as the fundamental principle of our democracy.

Political Diversity in Democracy

The term "democracy" was originated in Greece to
describe a government where people participate in
directing the affairs, of the State and in making its
laws. Pure democracy, however, did not exist in
Greece. There was always an aristocratic or oligarchic
basis for representation in the State. The masses
could only claim the power of criticism and judgment
of the government's policies and conduct. For Plato,
the participation of the masses in government, which
in extreme form becomes mob rule, and the
principles advocated by democracy, which include
equality of rights and freedom of speech, were only
sources of evil. Plato rejected democracy, while
Aristotle accepted it as a lesser evil. Where we have
mob rule, stated Aristotle, we have demagogues: "For
in cities governed democratically, but also legally,
there are no demagogues: the best among the citizens
take the lead." He warned that when "demagogues
come into play" democracy turns into tyranny.

The chief distinction that sets democracy apart from

totalitarian regimes is that it requires from its citizens and leaders tolerance of political diversity. Without tolerance, while permitting citizens to formulate their preferences, majority rule degenerates into a tyranny that imposes on them an oppressive yoke of uniformity in opinion and action. Citizens should also have unimpaired opportunities to change their preferences, which may be affected by multifarious causes, some laudable, some blamable. Preferences are continually changing because questions of social or political character may have new aspects in a rapidly changing society. History shows us that opinions in a certain period are often deemed false or unreasonable in a subsequent time. It is certain that some of our present preferences will be rejected by future ages. What should never be changed, however, is the guarantee, necessary for democracy, that the freedom of the individual to express his preferences will always be preserved.

In stressing that tolerance, demanding unrestrained freedom of discussion, is essential to democracy, John Stuart Mill wrote, "If all mankind minus one were of one opinion, mankind would be no more justified in silencing that person than he, if he had the power, would be justified in silencing mankind." Mill argued that silencing the expression of an opinion is doing more harm to those who dissent from the opinion than those who hold it. "If the opinion is right, they are deprived of the opportunity of exchanging error for truth; if wrong, they lose . . . the clearer perception and livelier impression of truth produced by its collision with error."

In a democracy, the "self-government" of the "people" does not mean the government of each by himself, but of each by an elective and responsible government. The will of the "people" does not mean the will of all the people but of the part of the people that succeeded in being accepted as the majority. To protect the individual from the tyranny of the majority, the holders of power remain accountable to all the people, and only through a free exchange of ideas and free debate can the wisdom of political decisions be carefully evaluated by every member of a democratic community who has the right to vote in a free and fair election.

Our representative form of government precludes "mob rule," or widespread participation in governing in a direct sense. The people have the "equality of rights and freedom of speech," which they use in deciding to accept or to refuse the men who are to rule them. The electorate has a free choice among the would-be leaders who compete for his vote. The competition is on issues and often on personality. Political tolerance, which is crucial for the voter's judgment, demands of the candidates an explanation of their positions on issues affecting the life of the nation and the welfare of its citizens. Their positions may be unpopular, but they express them without fear of reprisal. The debates of competing candidates have become a popular scene of action in American politics.

The "great" debates started with the Lincoln-Douglas joint appearances before the American public. Slavery was the vital subject of their political arguments, which attracted crowds too great for public halls, so the two rivals met in open groves. In this generation, millions of plain Americans watched the debates between Kennedy and Nixon, Carter and Ford, Carter and Reagan, and Reagan and Mondale. The content of the debates included such issues as foreign policy, inflation, the decline of the cities, oil and energy, social security, and other propositions, all revolving around the role of government, the safety of our nation, our economic stability, and the use of American power. The televised debates brought together in one audience millions of voters so as to give them the opportunity to choose their political leaders. By their choice, they expressed indirectly their opinions on the debate issues of their concern.

Through tolerance, which permits free debate and free exchange of ideas, government becomes responsive to the will of the people. The history of tolerance is the history of the triumph of truth over intolerance and falsehood. By persecution and intolerance, truth may be withheld from disclosure at one time or at many times, but in the course of the ages we find it rediscovered, generally accepted, and resistant to further attempts to suppress it. Silencing the free exchange of ideas is an assumption of infallibility.

How Much Tolerance?

We are not infallible, democracy is not perfect, and we cannot expect even perfect tolerance. This brings us back to the quesion, raised at the beginning of this lecture, of how much tolerance is justified to preserve a balance between tolerance and other values. What restraints can be placed on the extent of tolerance to protect society from infringing on its political liberties or rights? What are the rules of democratic restraint to prevent tolerance of intolerance from being utilized for antidemocratic purposes? When in a democracy is the government justified in prohibiting the promulgation of opinions dangerous to democracy or in restraining the right of demonstration with the purpose of undermining the foundation of public order?

The strain between tolerance and intolerance (or tolerance of intolerance) may be illustrated by two opinions of the Supreme Court—in each case, dissenting opinions from Justice Holmes and Brandeis, respectively. In the case of *Abrams v. United States* (250 U.S. 616, 617, 40 S.Ct. 17 [1919]), the defendants were charged with conspiring, when the United States was at war with Germany, to unlawfully utter, print, write, and publish "disloyal, scurrilous and abusive language about the form of government of the United States," to "incite, provoke and encourage resistance to the United States in said war," and to "incite and advocate curtailment of production of things and products necessary and essential to the prosecution of the war." After denouncing President Wilson as a hypocrite and a coward and assailing our government in general, the defendants appealed to the "workers" of this country to arise and put down by force the government of the United States as a "capitalistic enemy." The articles of the defendants contained a definite threat "to create so great a disturbance that the autocrats of America shall be compelled to keep their armies at home, and not be able to spare any for Russia." There was also a threat of armed rebellion. "If they will use arms against the Russian people to enforce their standard of order, so will we use arms, and they shall never see the ruin of the Russian Revolution."

The Supreme Court affirmed the judgment of the District Court for the Southern District of New York convicting the defendants of conspiring to violate provisions of the Espionage Act of Congress (of June 15, 1917, as amended by the Act of May 16, 1918). The plain purpose of their criminal conduct, stated the Court, was "to excite, at the supreme crisis of war, disaffection, sedition, riots, and, they hoped, revolution in this country for the purpose of embarrassing and if possible defeating the military plans of the government in Europe."

Justice Holmes in his dissent argued that the principle of the right to free speech is always the same, even against charges peculiar to war. "It is only the present danger of immediate evil or an intent to bring it about that warrants Congress in setting a limit to the expression of opinion where private rights are not concerned . . . Now nobody can suppose that the surreptitious publishing of a silly leaflet by an unknown man, without more, would present any immediate danger than its opinions would hinder the success of the government arms or have any appreciable tendency to do so." (250 U.S. 616, 628, 40 S.Ct. 17, 21 [1919].)

This lack of consensus over the direction of public

policy and over a definition of the limits of tolerance appeared also in the case of *Gitlow v. People of the State of New York*. Benjamin Gitlow was indicted for the statutory crime of criminal anarchy as defined by the New York Penal Code. The judgment was affirmed by the Court of Appeals. The defendant, a member of the Left Wing Section of the Socialist Party, advocated in a published "Manifesto" the destruction of the state and the establishment of the dictatorship of the proletariat by "organizing the industrial proletariat into militant Socialist unions and at the earliest opportunity through mass strike and force and violence, if necessary, compelling the government to cease to function, and then through a proletarian dictatorship, taking charge of and appropriating all property . . ." (268 U.S. 652, 662, 45 S.Ct. 625, 628 [1925].)

The Supreme Court affirmed the judgment of the Court of Appeals that held that the Manifesto "advocated the overthrow of the government by violence, or by unlawful means." It is a fundamental principle, stated the Supreme Court, that the freedom of speech and of the press "does not confer an absolute right to speak or publish, without responsibility, whatever one may choose, or an unrestricted and unbridled license that gives immunity for every possible use of language and prevents the punishment of those who abuse this freedom." Freedom of speech and of the press does not protect publications promoting the overthrow of the government by force or teachings which tend to subvert the government or to hinder it in the performance of its duties. The State, according to the Supreme Court, is the primary judge of regulations required in the interest of public safety and welfare, and its statutes may be declared unconstitutional only when they are arbitrary and unreasonable.

Justice Holmes, in his dissenting opinion, agreed that the test sanctioned by the full Court in *Schenck v. United States* (249 U.S. 47, 52, 39 S.Ct. 247 249 [1919]) applied in this case. The often-reiterated "clear and present danger" test is whether the words are used in such circumstances and are of such a nature as to create a clear and present danger that they will bring about the substantive evils that the State has a right to prevent. In Holmes' judgment, "If in the long run the beliefs expressed in proletarian dictatorship are destined to be accepted by the dominant forces of the community, the only meaning of free speech is that they should be given their chance and have their way." (*Gitlow v. People of the State of New York*, 268 U.S. 652, 673 45 S.Ct. 625, 632 [1925].) Furthermore, the publication of the Manifesto, he stated, did not attempt to induce an uprising against the government at once but at some indefinite time in the future, and, therefore, it was too remote from possible consequences.

Necessary Measures

What is the main point of the differences in opinions on tolerance expressed above, differences that may have great consequences for the preservation of our democratic form of government? History shows us that utterances inciting the overthrow of an organized, duly elected government may kindle a spark that while smoldering for a time may break open with sudden violence into a sweeping and destructive fire. The Supreme Court has taken the position that the State cannot reasonably be required to measure the danger from every such utterance "in the nice balance of a jeweler's scale." The State is not acting arbitrarily or unreasonably when it takes measures necessary to extinguish this spark without waiting until it blazes into a conflagration.

As the Illinois Supreme Court explained in another case, *People v. Lloyd* (304 Ill. 23, 35, 136, N.E. 501, 512), the State has the authority to forbid the advocacy of a doctrine intended to overthrow the government without waiting until there is a present and imminent danger of the success of the advocated plan. "If the State were compelled to wait until the apprehended danger became certain, then its right to protect itself would come into being simultaneously with the overthrow of the government, when there would be neither prosecuting officers nor courts for the enforcement of the law."

For Justice Holmes, the danger of bringing about the "substantive evil" must be present and imminent and not too "remote from possible consequences." His dissenting opinions, quoted above, do not reflect the legal pragmatism advocated by Holmes, a pragmatism that was the prominent feature of his great work, *The Common Law*. Holmes rejected the concept of abstract justice when he wrote "that the Common Law is not a brooding omnipresence in the sky" and "the U.S. is not subject to the mystic overlaw that it is bound to obey." Because of the "felt necessities," he stated, the right of free speech must be denied to a mischievous person falsely crying "Fire" in a crowded theatre and should be limited in time of war.

Adhering to the historic school of jurisprudence, he wrote:

> "The life of the law has not been logic: it has been experience. The felt necessities of the time, the prevalent moral and political theories, intuitions of public policy, avowed or unconscious, even the prejudices which judges share with their fellow-men have had a good deal more to do than the syllogism in determining the rules by which men should be governed . . . The substance of the law at any given time pretty nearly corresponds, so far as it goes, with what is then understood to be convenient." (*The Common Law*, Little, Brown, and Company, 1881, p. 5.)

As a pragmatist Holmes urged others to face realistically the political and social problems in a rapidly changing society. Obviously, when writing in 1919 and 1925 his dissenting opinions in the cases of *Abrams* and *Gitlow*, which we have been discussing, he could not foresee how deep human depravity brought on by communism and nazism could go. Nor did the Supreme Court give consideration to the extent of this depravity by making a distinction in numerous cases between mere advocacy of forcible overthrow of government and preparing a group for violent action or steeling it to such action.

Faith in the Democratic Process

In the perspective of historical developments and of the tragedies the world has experienced under the yoke of totalitarian regimes, the conclusion to be reached is: A democratic State should exercise its police power to punish those who abuse freedom of speech and of the press by utterance tending to disturb public peace and order, to corrupt public morals, and to incite to crime. The democratic State has the duty to protect its primary and essential right of preservation and has the authority to judge the regulations required in the interest of public safety and welfare. In our independent courts was vested the responsibility to resist every unreasonable encroachment upon the rights of the individual stipulated for in the Constituiton by its declaration of rights. Due process protects the individual against arbitrary and capricious actions of the government.

This conclusion is also pertinent to the question of what restraints should be placed on the extent of tolerance to protect the public from the abuse of the right of the people "peaceably" to assemble. It is the authority of the State or the local government, which represent the free choice of democratic and law-abiding citizens, to prevent or punish where "clear and present danger" of rioting, burning, looting, and of any other public disorder appears or presents an immediate threat to peace and public safety. States and cities should be sustained in this power in order for the people not to lose faith in the democratic process of free choice of their governments. Freedom of assembly exists under the law and not independently of it.

The strategy of mass demonstrations as used by groups resorting to terror tactics was summed up by Hitler: "We should not work in secret conventicles but in mighty mass demonstrations, and it is not by dagger and poison or pistol that the road can be cleared for the movement but by the conquest of the streets." (Quoted from Justice Jackson's dissenting opinion in *Terminello v. City of Chicago*, 337 U.S. 1, 23, 69 S.Ct. 894, 904 [1949].) Our constitutional rights will be endangered if we do not have protection from abuses which lead to violence and destruction. The rights of free speech and assembly do not mean that everyone with opinions and beliefs has the right to say what he pleases or to engage in demonstrations where he pleases and when he pleases. It is a myth to consider such rights as constitutional.

Civil liberty does not mean removal of all restraints from those who abuse this liberty and advocate the evil of intolerance. It cannot be stressed enough, however, that the power to prevent any conduct which induces people to violate the law cannot be invoked in bad faith, as a cover for suppression or censorship, which is in direct conflict with the kind of government envisioned by those who adopted our Bill of Rights. The holders of power remain always accountable to their communities. In a democracy, the people demand from their governments a policy of tolerance, since communication with one another and exchange of ideas constitute the basis of all common achievement.

Democracy flourishes in a free market of ideas where truth gets itself accepted in the competition provided by the free trade of ideas visualized by the

Framers of the Constitution. Society must, therefore, be vigorously protected against self-appointed "heralds of truth" who can do to the public as much or more harm as if the allegedly harmful ideas they are trying to suppress are tolerated. In diversity of opinion, stated John Stuart Mill, is the only "chance of a fair play to all sides of the truth." Free discussion cannot be denied, and the right of criticism must not be stifled. The worst offense which can be committed by a polemic "is to stigmatize those who hold the contrary opinion as bad and immoral men."

In my book *Three Sources of National Strength*, I listed tolerance as one of the important elements of patriotism. I pointed out that one of the abuses of patriotism is to use it as a club to attack fellow citizens who differ in their opinions from oneself. The welfare of our society is endangered when those who proclaim themselves patriots attack the patriotism of faithful public servants and irresponsibly attempt to destroy the harmony of society by seeing treason in all dissidence. The deepest sense of patriotism is betrayed by those who by self-assertion, belligerence, and hatred impugn the motives of others. I wrote,

> "If one claims that his opinion is the voice of God and condemns all whose opinions differ from his own, then God has actually been left out of the picture. . . . Mutual tolerance is the inner light in which freedom lives and grows, it is the air from which man draws the breath of love for his country." (The University of Texas at Dallas, 1986, p. 148.)

Arthur Miller, in a note to the first act of *The Crucible*, emphasizes the danger in irresponsible suppression of dissidence:

"In the countries of the Communist ideology, all resistance of any import is linked to the totally malign capitalist succubi, and in America any man who is not reactionary in his views is open to the charge of alliance with the Red hell. Political opposition, thereby, is given an inhumane overlay which then justifies the abrogation of all normally applied customs of civilized intercourse. A political policy is equated with moral right, and opposition to it with diabolical malevolence. Once such an equation is effectively made, society becomes a congeries of plots and counterplots, and the main role of government changes from that of the arbiter to that of the scourge of God." (Viking Press, 1954, p. 34.)

Our nation has repeatedly struggled against the forces of intolerance. History reminds us that in the United States intolerance—manifesting itself in the garb of loyalty, with all its attendant overzealous partisanship and witch-hunting—was behind the infamous Alien and Sedition Laws of 1798 (the Alien Law passed on June 25 and the Sedition law on July 14, but usually they are named together), the Sedition Act of 1918, and the so-called McCarthy period (1950-1954). The infamous Alien and Sedition Laws of 1798 passed because of the fear that French Liberalism and an alliance between the French and the leaders of the

Republican Party would endanger the Federalist party's programs.

The Alien Act gave the President power to banish from the country any alien whom he judged suspicious, without giving a reason and without conducting a trial of any sort. The Sedition Act made it a crime, punishable by fine and imprisonment, to be found guilty of "combining and conspiring to oppose the execution of the laws, or publishing false or malicious writings against the President, Congress, or the government of the United States." The Sedition Act was aimed chiefly at Republican newspapers.

President Adams made no use of the law empowering him to expel dangerous aliens and the Alien Law was never enforced; it expired unused two years after its enactment. Not so with the Sedition Act. The arrest of editors who criticized the government proved to be a boomerang to the Federalists. The Sedition Act, intended to release partisan bitterness, helped to unite the opposition and unified the party that had framed it. The Republicans, as their answer, drafted the Kentucky and Virginia Resolutions, which were designed to awake the people to the fact that the Alien and Sedition Acts were unconstitutional, since the government had overstepped its rightful authority in passing them. The Federalist party suffered a defeat in the presidential election, and when Jefferson took office in 1801, he pardoned all who were prisoners under the Sedition Law.

The doctrine of sedition was revived by the Sedition Act of 1918, which extended the offenses covered by the Espionage Act of 1917 so as to cover disloyal utterances against the government, the Constitution, the military uniform, or the flag, and went far toward abolishing freedom of speech and the press. The Postmaster General was given arbitrary power to exclude from the mail publications which seemed to violate the provisions of the sedition laws. A generation later, the so-called McCarthy period marked as targets of a witch-hunt persons suspected of disloyal intentions; such a moral climate did not generate patriotic fervor and loyalty but only intensified mutual suspicion.

As we have seen, over the years important Supreme Court decisions have discouraged attempts to constitutionalize intolerance under the guise of protecting loyalty by greatly reducing the range of constitutionally valid legislation aimed at punishing alleged disloyalty. The Court has repeatedly stressed that the liberty protected by the Constitution may not be interfered with, under the guise of protecting the public interest, by legislative action which is arbitrary or without reasonable relation to some purpose within the competency of the government to effect.

Tolerance is an indispensable quality in a democracy since it enables people of different origins, races, and religions to live together and to work together in the spirit of building an orderly society. Tolerance is a powerful medicine in a society built on the premises of individual dignity, freedom of choice, and the right to criticize public men and measures— as long as the means used are peaceful. Discord is not a sign of weakness but of strength, a sign of meaningful participation of the citizenry in the political process. Such participation must not be required to meet arbitrary standards of acceptability. We should be eternally vigilant against attempts to restrain open debate from challenging deep-seated beliefs because of fear of resentment.

Tolerance opens broader enduring values than the ones offered by "sacred" patterns dictated by those who claim a monopoly of rectitude and righteousness. A democratic society grows in wisdom by constant scrutiny of thought and ideas, and as it grows in capacity for liberty, the spirit of tolerance will grow in its citizens.

JC
423
.D4416
1988

JC
423
.D4416

1988

16.50